Understanding East Asia's Economic "Miracles"

Front cover images:

Top left: 500 series shinkansen set W1 passing Maibara Station on the "Nozomi 29" service, Japan. Source: https://commons.wikimedia.org/wiki/File:JRW_Shinkansen_Series_500_W1_sets.jpg

Top right: Gangnam district, Seoul, Korea. Source: https://commons.wikimedia.org/wiki/File:Seoul_picture.jpg

Bottom right: Dragon and Tiger Pagodas, Kaohsiung, Taiwan.
Source: https://commons.wikimedia.org/wiki/File:Dragon_and_Tiger_Pagodas_03.jpg

Bottom left: Suzhou Creek Shanghai, China. Source: https://commons.wikimedia.org/wiki/File:Suzhou_Creek_From_General_Post_Office_2011.jpg

Back cover image:

Shinjuku, Tokyo, Japan, at night: Traffic on Ōme-kaidō.
Source: https://commons.wikimedia.org/wiki/File:Night_in_Shinjuku_3.JPG

Key Issues in Asian Studies, No. 3

AAS Resources for Teaching About Asia

Understanding East Asia's Economic "Miracles"

Zhiqun Zhu

Association for Asian Studies, Inc.
825 Victors Way, Suite 310
Ann Arbor, MI 48108 USA
www.asian-studies.org

KEY ISSUES IN ASIAN STUDIES
Lucien Ellington, University of Tennessee at Chattanooga, Editor

"Key Issues" booklets complement the Association for Asian Studies teaching journal, *Education About Asia*—a practical teaching resource for secondary school, college, and university instructors, as well as an invaluable source of information for students, scholars, libraries, and those who have an interest in Asia.

Formed in 1941, **the Association for Asian Studies (AAS)**—the largest society of its kind, with more than 8,000 members worldwide—is a scholarly, non-political, non-profit professional association open to all persons interested in Asia.

For further information, please visit www.asian-studies.org

Originally printed in 2009. Second printing: 2012.

This revised and expanded edition printed in 2016.

ISBN for 2016 edition: 978-0-924304-79-8.

Published by:
Association for Asian Studies, Inc.
825 Victors Way, Suite 310, Ann Arbor, Michigan 48108 USA
www.asian-studies.org

The Library of Congress has cataloged this booklet as:

Zhu, Zhiqun.
Understanding East Asia's economic miracles / Zhiqun Zhu.
    p. cm. — (Key issues in Asian studies ; no. 3)
Includes bibliographical references.
ISBN 978-0-924304-54-5 (pbk.: alk. paper) 1. East Asia—Economic conditions—Case studies. 2. East Asia—Economic policy—Case studies. I. Title.

HC460.5.Z545 2009
330.95--dc22

                              2009006197

ABOUT THE AUTHOR

Zhiqun Zhu, PhD, is currently an associate professor of political science and international relations and inaugural director of the China Institute at Bucknell University. He was Bucknell's MacArthur Chair in East Asian politics from 2008 to 2014. He has also taught at University of Bridgeport, Hamilton College, University of South Carolina, and Shanghai International Studies University. In the early 1990s, he was Senior Assistant to Consul for Press and Cultural Affairs at the American Consulate General in Shanghai.

Dr. Zhu's teaching and research interests include Chinese politics and foreign policy, East Asian security, and US-China relations. He is the author and editor of over 10 books, including *China's New Diplomacy: Rationale, Strategies and Significance* (Ashgate, 2013); *New Dynamics in East Asian Politics: Security, Political Economy, and Society* (Continuum International, 2012); and *US-China Relations in the 21st Century: Power Transition and Peace* (Routledge, 2005).

Professor Zhu has received several research fellowships, including two POSCO fellowships at the East-West Center in Hawaii, a Korea Foundation/ Freeman Foundation fellowship to do research in Korea, two visiting fellowships at the East Asian Institute of National University of Singapore, and a visiting professorship at Doshisha University in Kyoto, Japan. He is a member of the National Committee on United States-China Relations and is frequently sought by international media to comment on Chinese and East Asian affairs.

About "Key Issues in Asian Studies"

Key Issues in Asian Studies (*KIAS*) volumes engage major cultural and historical themes in the Asian experience. *Key Issues* books complement the Association for Asian Studies' teaching journal, *Education About Asia*, and serve as vital educational materials that are both accessible and affordable for classroom use.

Key Issues books tackle broad subjects or major events in an introductory but compelling style appropriate for survey courses. Although authors of the series have distinguished themselves as scholars as well as teachers, the prose style employed is accessible for broad audiences. This series is intended for teachers and undergraduates at two- and four-year colleges as well as advanced high school students and secondary school teachers engaged in teaching Asian studies in a comparative framework and anyone with an interest in Asia.

For further information visit www.asian-studies.org.

Prospective authors interested in *Key Issues in Asian Studies* or *Education About Asia* are encouraged to contact Lucien Ellington, University of Tennessee at Chattanooga; Tel: (423) 425-2118; E-Mail: Lucien-Ellington@utc.edu.

"Key Issues" volumes available from AAS:

Japanese Literature: From Murasaki to Murakami by Marvin Marcus

Japan Since 1945 by Paul E. Dunscomb

East Asian Societies by W. Lawrence Neuman

Confucius in East Asia by Jeffrey L. Richey

The Story of Việt Nam: From Prehistory to the Present by Shelton Woods

Modern Chinese History by David Kenley

Korea in World History by Donald N. Clark

Traditional China in Asian and World History by Tansen Sen and Victor Mair

Zen Past and Present by Eric Cunningham

Japan and Imperialism, 1853–1945 by James L. Huffman

Japanese Popular Culture and Globalization by William M. Tsutsui

Global India circa 100 CE: South Asia in Early World History by Richard H. Davis

Caste in India by Diane Mines

Understanding East Asia's Economic "Miracles" by Zhiqun Zhu

Political Rights in Post-Mao China by Merle Goldman

Gender, Sexuality, and Body Politics in Modern Asia by Michael Peletz

Preface to the 2016 Edition

Much has changed in East Asia since this booklet was first published in 2009. In Japan, the political revolving door at the top has produced six prime ministers since 2006, making it hard for Japan to have consistent policies to seriously deal with its sluggish economic recovery. A massive 9.0-magnitude earthquake struck northern Japan, triggering a devastating tsunami in March 2011. More than 20,000 people were killed or missing. The Fukushima nuclear reactors were damaged, causing radiation leaks. These triple disasters added fuel to the fire in Japan's efforts to recover. Abe Shinzo who returned to office in December 2012 attempted to revamp the Japanese economy through his ambitious Abenomics, but without much success. Critics say that he focused too much on defense issues such as forcing a national security bill through the Diet in 2015. Tokyo's hosting of the 2020 Summer Olympics and Japan's participation in the Trans-Pacific Partnership (TPP) hopefully will provide new impetus for Japan's recovery.

In China, the economy that surpassed Japan's as the world's second largest in 2010 has slowed down since 2012. This rising power faces daunting problems and challenges such as a widening income gap, growing social protests, rampant corruption, and a worsening environment. Xi Jinping has emerged as a strong and assertive leader both domestically and internationally. While his anti-corruption campaign has won widespread support, Xi faces tremendous oppositions from within the Party, the military and state-owned enterprises (SOEs) in political and economic reforms. In Taiwan, Ma Ying-jeou's 8 years in office as the ROC president brought stability and economic cooperation across the Taiwan Strait. Taiwan and mainland China signed the historic Economic Cooperation Framework Agreement (ECFA) in 2010, ushering in a new chapter in cross-Strait relations. Ma and Xi held a historic meeting in Singapore in November 2015. However, no political breakthrough is likely in the near future, and the Taiwanese society remains highly divided over Taiwan's relations with mainland China. As the DPP prepares to return to power in 2016, cross-Strait relations have entered a new era of uncertainty.

On the Korean Peninsula, North Korea formally pulled out of the Six-Party talks in 2009. Kim Jong-il, who ruled North Korea since 1994, died at the end of 2011. His youngest son, the twenty-something Kim Jong-un, succeeded him, raising concerns about whether the inexperienced younger Kim can maintain stability of North Korea. Some had hoped that Kim Jong-un, who studied in Switzerland as a teenager, might introduce economic and political reforms to

North Korea after he consolidated power. As of 2016, North Korea remained defiant and refused to give up its nuclear program. In the South, the ROK-US and ROK-China free trade agreements took effect in 2012 and 2015 respectively, further boosting South Korea's trade with the US and China. President Park Geun-hye, daughter of former president Park Chung-hee, came to office in 2013 as the first woman president of the ROK and took a more balanced approach toward the United States and China, maintaining strong relations with both powers.

At the end of 2015, the US-led TPP successfully concluded its negotiations with the United States, Japan, and other 10 Pacific economies as members. The TPP faces stiff opposition in some member states. South Korea, Taiwan, and the PRC hope to join the trade agreement in the future. However, political tensions in Northeast Asia have prevented Japan, South Korea and China from moving forward with their proposed trilateral free trade agreement.

Such new developments require the booklet to be updated and slightly revised. This updated edition also includes a glossary and an expanded "Suggestions for Further Reading", but the basic thesis and argument in the book remain the same. I hope that students and other readers will benefit from this updated version.

Zhiqun Zhu
Lewisburg, Pennsylvania
March 2016

Editor's Introduction

This is the third time that I have had the privilege of working with Professor Zhiqun Zhu on the development of the volume, *Understanding East Asia's Economic "Miracles."* In this version, the author updates developments since 2012 for the four polities included in the booklet. A number of important events have occurred in post-World War II Asia but in terms of dramatic improvements in the quality of now billions of people's lives, no story since 1945 is as important as the so-called East Asian economic "miracles." The rapid development began in Japan, and then occurred in South Korea, Hong Kong, Taiwan, and Singapore. By the 1970s with the end of the Mao era, economic liberalization began in earnest in China, and by the 1990s other Asian nations, including Asia's second giant, India, adopted some of the key policies that caused East Asia to have the most unprecedented economic growth since the industrial revolutions of the 19th century.

The reason that instructors and students now have a second edition (there was an updated 2012 second printing) is that Professor Zhu manages to demystify the "miracle" jargon by telling the stories, in lucid, accurate and well-written prose of the sometimes similar but often different economic trajectories of Japan, South Korea, Taiwan, and the People's Republic of China. He even-handedly describes the roles of private enterprise and government during the sea changes that occurred in East Asia and objectively introduces controversial topics upon which scholars disagree. Professor Zhu also illumines readers on the weaknesses as well as the strengths of the economic systems that politicians, elite bureaucrats, and last but not least, resourceful entrepreneurs and hard-working ordinary people created. This is a booklet that in my opinion is the ideal basic reading for students or their instructors who know little about the topic.

This second edition would not have been possible without the helpful comments that shaped the first edition. I am grateful to Robert Angel, Andrew Oros, and Richard Rice who served as reviewers of the first edition, to AAS Publications Manager, Jon Wilson who worked on all three versions of the booklet and last but not least to the AAS Editorial Board (and in particular, Bill Tsutsui.)

Lucien Ellington
Series Editor: Key Issues in Asian Studies

Acknowledgements

I am grateful to a number of people who have helped me to make the publication of this booklet possible. First of all, I wish to thank Lucien Ellington, Editor of *Education About Asia* and the "Key Issues in Asian Studies" (KIAS) series, for finding the value in my proposal and for encouraging me to take up the challenge to write the booklet. I am very fortunate to have worked with Lucien and to publish the first booklet in the *KIAS* series under his editorship.

Jon Wilson, Publications and Website Manager of the Association for Asian Studies, has overseen the publication of the booklet and has been extremely responsive, meticulous, and efficient. It has truly been my great pleasure to work with Jon. Janet Opdyke, copyeditor for the booklet, carefully read through the manuscript and polished it. Janet's hard work definitely makes the booklet more readable. Professor Xiaoyu Pu made some good suggestions for revising the text. I also wish to thank the three reviewers for their useful comments and helpful suggestions. All the above individuals have helped to improve the quality of the booklet, but they are not responsible for any mistakes.

As usual, my family has been very patient and supportive during my writing of this booklet. Zhimin, Julia, Sophia, and Matthew bring me much love and joy every day. I am lucky to have their unconditional support.

Zhiqun Zhu
Lewisburg, Pennsylvania
March 2016

CONTENTS

LIST OF ABBREVIATIONS

AIIB	Asian Infrastructure Investment Bank
APEC	Asia-Pacific Economic Cooperation
CNOOC	China National Offshore Oil Company, Ltd.
DPJ	Democratic Party of Japan
DPP	Democratic Progressive Party
DPRK	Democratic People's Republic of Korea
ECFA	Economic Cooperation Framework Agreement
FDI	foreign direct investment
FILP	Fiscal Investment and Loan Plan
GATT	General Agreement on Tariffs and Trade
GDP	gross domestic product
GNP	gross national product
IMD	International Institute for Management Development
IMF	International Monetary Fund
IPO	initial public offering
IT	information technology
JCRR	Joint Commission on Rural Reconstruction
KMT	Kuomintang
LCD	liquid crystal display
LDP	Liberal Democratic Party
MCI	Ministry of Commerce and Industry
METI	Ministry of Economy, Trade, and Industry
MITI	Ministry of International Trade and Industry
MM	Ministry of Munitions
MOF	Ministry of Finance
NIE	newly industrializing economy
OECD	Organization for Economic Cooperation and Development
PPP	purchasing power parity

PRC	People's Republic of China
ROC	Republic of China
ROK	Republic of Korea
SCAP	Supreme Commander of the Allied Powers
SDR	Special Drawing Rights
SEZ	special economic zone
SME	small and medium enterprise
SOE	state-owned enterprise
TPP	Trans-Pacific Partnership
TRA	Taiwan Relations Act
TVE	township and village enterprise
UNCTAD	United Nations Conference on Trade and Development
UNESCO	United Nations Educational, Scientific, and Cultural Organization
UNIKOTECH	Unification of Korean Technologies
WHO	World Health Organization
WTO	World Trade Organization

MODERN EAST ASIAN HISTORY TIMELINE

1839–42	First Opium War
1853–54	Commodore Matthew Perry visits Japan
1868	Meiji Restoration begins in Japan
1894–95	First Sino-Japanese War
1895	Japan defeats Qing dynasty China and colonizes Taiwan
1904–05	Russo-Japanese War
1910	Japan colonizes the Korean Peninsula, Korea's Choson dynasty ends
1911	Republic of China is established
1931	Japan creates the puppet state of Manchukuo in Manchuria
1937	Japan invades China and captures the capital city of Nanjing
1945	Japan surrenders at the end of World War II
	Chinese Civil War resumes
1947	Japan ratifies a new constitution and adopts land reform
1948	Republic of Korea (ROK) and the Democratic People's Republic of Korea (DPRK) are established
1949	People's Republic of China (PRC) is established
	Ministry of International Trade and Industry (MITI) is formed in Japan
	Land reform begins in Taiwan
1950–53	Korean War
1955	Japan's Liberal Democratic Party (LDP) is formed
1958–61	"Great Leap Forward" in China
1964	Tokyo Summer Olympics
1966–76	"Cultural Revolution" in China
1971	PRC enters the United Nations, replacing Taiwan
1972	United States returns Okinawa to Japan
	President Richard Nixon visits China

1978	Deng Xiaoping's reform and opening-up policies are implemented
1979	Four Special Economic Zones (SEZ) are established in Southern China
	PRC and the U.S. establish diplomatic relations
1980	Kwangju uprising in South Korea
1987	Martial law is lifted in Taiwan
1988	Seoul Summer Olympics
1989	Tiananmen Square demonstrations
	Asia-Pacific Economic Cooperation (APEC) is founded
1990s	Famines in North Korea
1991	Japanese economic "bubble" bursts, initiating the "lost decade"
1996	South Korea is admitted to the Organization for Economic Cooperation and Development (OECD)
1997	Asian financial crisis
	Hong Kong is returned to China
2000	Kuomintang loses power to the Democratic Progressive Party (DPP) in Taiwan
	First Inter-Korean Summit between South Korean President Kim Dae-jung and North Korean leader Kim Jong-il
2001	China enters the World Trade Organization (WTO)
	Ministry of Economy, Trade, and Industry (METI) replaces MITI
2003	Six-Party Talks over North Korea's nuclear program are launched in Beijing
2004	Protection of private property is written into the Chinese Constitution
2005	Agricultural taxes—which have existed for two-thousand years— are abolished in China
2007	The PRC Property Law goes into effect
	The Liberal Democratic Party (LDP) loses majority in upper house of the Japanese Diet
2007–08	South Koreans protest U.S.-ROK free trade agreement and U.S. beef imports

2008	Beijing Summer Olympics
	Global financial crisis
	The Chinese mainland and Taiwan start direct air and sea transport and postal services—the first time since the two sides split after the civil war in 1949
	Former ROC President Chen Shui-bian is arrested and indicted for forgery, money-laundering, and the misuse of public funds
2009	China announces its plan to begin providing health care to much of its population and to achieve universal health care by 2020.
	The Democratic Party of Japan (DPJ) becomes Japan's ruling party after defeating the long-dominant Liberal Democratic Party (LDP) in the parliamentary election.
2010	China replaces Japan to become the world's second largest economy.
	The World Expo is held in Shanghai.
	The historic Economic Cooperation Framework Agreement (ECFA) is signed between mainland China and Taiwan.
	ROK navy ship *Cheonan* is sunk, presumably by North Korea. North Korea attacks the island of *Yeonpyeong* in South Korea.
2011	A massive 9.0-magnitude earthquake strikes northeast Japan, triggering a devastating tsunami. Approximately 20,000 people are killed or missing. The Fukushima nuclear reactors are damaged, causing radiation leaks.
	Noda Yoshihiko becomes Japan's sixth prime minister since 2006.
	North Korean leader Kim Jong-il dies. His youngest son Kim Jong-un assumes power.
2012	KMT's Ma Ying-jeou is reelected as the ROC president.
	China and Japan agree to help solve the eurozone debt crisis.
	The Chinese Communist Party holds its 18th national congress, selecting a new generation of leaders.
	ROK-US free trade agreement takes effect.

2013	Xi Jinping becomes PRC president and proposes "One Belt, One Road" development strategies.
	Prime Minister Abe Shinzo visits the Yasukuni Shrine after returning to power the year before.
	China declares an Air Defense Identification Zone (ADIZ) in East China Sea.
	Park Geun-hye becomes the first female president of the ROK.
2014	Sunflower Student Movement in Taiwan
	"Occupy Central" pro-democracy protests in Hong Kong
	APEC summit in Beijing
2015	TPP agreement is reached among twelve Pacific Rim economies.
	Asian Infrastructure Investment Bank (AIIB) is formed.
	China's "one child policy" is abolished.
	ROK-PRC free trade agreement takes effect.
	Renminbi joins the IMF's Special Drawing Rights basket of reserve currencies.
	Xi Jinping and Ma Ying-jeou meet in Singapore.
2016	North Korea tests a hydrogen bomb and launches a satellite. The UN imposes the toughest ever sanctions against North Korea.
	The Bank of Japan adopts negative interest rates to stimulate commercial lending and spending.
	Tsai Ing-wen becomes the first female president of the ROC.

1

INTRODUCTION

S ince the end of World War II no region in the world has been as dynamic as East Asia, where one nation after another has created remarkable economic and political "miracles." First Japan rose from the devastation of the Pacific War like a phoenix coming back to life and quickly demilitarized and democratized and became the second-largest economy in the world in the late 1960s, next only to the United States. Then the Republic of Korea (ROK or South Korea) and Taiwan, both former colonies of Japan, experienced economic takeoffs under authoritarian regimes before moving toward full democracy, achieving both economic and political marvels in a relatively short period of time by the late 1980s. Finally, in the late 1970s Deng Xiaoping, realizing that China was falling far behind many of its neighbors in living standards, decided to initiate market reforms in the countryside and gradually opened China's door to Western investment and technology, policies that pushed China onto a fast development track and helped turn it into an economic powerhouse at the beginning of the twenty-first century. Though China remains an authoritarian regime politically, its society has become highly diverse and pluralistic. Collectively, East Asia's impressive economic growth and social progress achieved in the seven decades after World War II are unparalleled in human history.

The word "miracle" suggests some sort of divine intervention. In East Asia, there has been no such divine power. East Asia's economic "miracles" have come from decades of hard work by the people of East Asia. These achievements have also been helped by favorable international and domestic conditions, sound government policies, and far-sighted individual leaders.

The so-called "flying geese pattern" vividly describes the post–World War II economic development of East Asia, with Japan as the leading goose followed by the four "little dragons" or "little tigers" (South Korea, Taiwan, Singapore, and Hong Kong) and other economies. In 1960, Japan and the rest of Asia accounted for only 5 percent of the world's gross national product (GNP) compared to 37 percent for North America. By the early twenty-first century, they had accounted for roughly 30 percent of world GNP, about the same share as those held by North America and Europe. By mid-century, Asia's economic size will be larger than that of North America or Europe.

China's profound economic and social transformations since the late 1970s, especially its spectacular surge in the first decade of the twenty-first century, have reignited scholarly and policy interest in East Asia's development models. Has China followed the same development trajectory as other East Asian economies? Is the People's Republic of China (PRC) replaying the East Asian "miracles" performed earlier by Japan, South Korea, Taiwan, and others?

Despite the extraordinary economic growth of post–World War II East Asia, what happened in the 1990s cast considerable doubt on the vitality of the often touted "East Asian model." Japan's long economic stagnation that began in the early 1990s and the 1997–98 financial crisis in some of the East Asian and Southeast Asian economies led many people to ask what went wrong with the highly regarded development miracles in East Asia. Is such a development model sustainable? What is the current status of these economies? Are global resources sufficient to maintain further growth in East Asia and elsewhere?

This booklet, through an historical and comparative study of the economic performances of Japan, South Korea, and China (including both mainland China and Taiwan), examines all the major explanations and analyses in accounting for East Asia's economic "miracles." It also discusses the implications for other developing economies as they emulate East Asia's success story. It is intended to help readers better understand the East Asian development experience, with both its strengths and weaknesses.

What powerful political, economic, and social forces have fueled East Asia's rapid growth since World War II? Is there a singular East Asian model of economic development? What are the differences and similarities in the development paths of Japan, South Korea, Taiwan, and the PRC? What is the relationship between economic growth and type of political regime? Can East Asia's high-performing development strategies be copied by other developing regions? This booklet provides a comprehensive survey of East Asian nations' post-World War II development from historical, cultural, institutional, political, economic, and international perspectives.

It will be helpful for understanding these successful economies and the driving forces behind them as well as serious challenges they face today. It will also be significant for other developing nations as they attempt to mimic East Asia's growth trajectory.

This booklet can be used at a variety of lower-level undergraduate classes in political science, international relations, economics, development studies, world history, geography, and Asian studies. It will be especially germane to introductory or survey courses such as East Asian Political Economy, Comparative Politics of East Asia, and Modern East Asian History. Since it has been written as an introductory reading on the topic, it should also be appropriate for advanced high school classes such as advanced placement (AP) courses in world history, comparative politics and government, and economics.

"Diverse" and "dynamic" are two distinctive features of East Asian nations. To understand these economies, it is important first of all to recognize that, although they enjoy some similarities in economic strategies, they differ greatly in their physical sizes, economic histories, political systems, political cultures, and foreign relations. An analysis of both internal and external factors is needed to explain East Asia's economic "miracles" after World War II. Chapters 2 through 4 examine post–World War II development in Japan, the Korean Peninsula, and China and Taiwan. Chapter 5 systematically compares and contrasts these cases. Chapter 6 summarizes the discussion and develops a comprehensive framework for better understanding the economic "miracles" of East Asia.

2

JAPAN AND THE "DEVELOPMENTAL STATE" MODEL

J apan was a relatively closed society in the first half of the nineteenth century. American Commodore Matthew C. Perry's July 1853 and February 1854 visits to Japan marked the official, albeit forced, opening of Japan to American and Western trade and influence. Through the Convention of Kanagawa and the subsequent United States–Japan Treaty of Amity and Commerce, America's gunboat diplomacy helped integrate Japan into the Western world and create a future economic giant in the East.

In an effort to avoid the fate of colonization or exploitation that China was suffering, Japan launched an ambitious drive to industrialize and modernize. The Meiji Restoration, which began in 1868, was in effect Japan's modernization and industrialization movement. Under the slogan "Enrich the country, strengthen the military" (*fukoku kyōhei*, 富国強兵), Japan mobilized all its resources and quickly rose to become a military power by the end of the nineteenth century. The Japanese economy was no longer predominantly agricultural, and Japan easily defeated an enfeebled and declining Qing dynasty China in the first Sino-Japanese War (1894–95), which permanently changed the power structure in East Asia and accelerated the fall of the last dynasty in China. With the signing of the Treaty of Shimonoseki, Japan took Taiwan as its colony until it surrendered in 1945. Meiji leaders' aim to turn the country into a power equal to the West had become a reality by the early twentieth century.

Japan was essentially given a free hand to grow and expand as the European powers were busy competing with one another while the United States stood on the sidelines of great power politics at the end of the nineteenth century and the beginning of the twentieth. Japan's ambitions in Manchuria and Korea collided with those of Russia, a great Eurasian power. Japan's fledgling navy surprisingly defeated Russia in the

Shinto Shrine in Atomic Ruins, Nagasaki, Japan, October 1945. Photo courtesy U.S. Marine Corps.

Russo-Japanese War (1904–05). In the Treaty of Portsmouth, signed on September 5, 1905, Russia recognized the Korean Peninsula as part of the Japanese sphere of influence and agreed to evacuate Manchuria. Japan annexed Korea in 1910 with scant protest from other powers. In World War I, Japan seized German possessions in Asia, including the Shandong Peninsula in China. In 1931, Japan invaded Manchuria and established the puppet government of Manchukuo (*Manzhouguo* 满洲国). By 1937, Japan had occupied many other parts of China, including the capital city of Nanjing (Nanking). It also invaded much of Southeast Asia in an attempt to create a "Greater East Asia Co-prosperity Sphere."

The Pacific War, with the participation of the United States, ended Japan's military expansionism, which had brought disaster to much of Asia, including Japan itself. The United States dropped atomic bombs on Hiroshima and Nagasaki on August 6 and August 9, 1945, respectively, leading to Japan's official surrender to the Allied Powers on August 15, 1945.

Japan's economic reconstruction began shortly after the war. However, to label the country's high growth rate following World War II a "miracle" underrates the transformation of Japan's economy which began in the nineteenth century and the expansion of heavy industry during the 1930s. Japan already had a highly developed military and industry before World War II, which distinguished it from other East Asian countries. It is not surprising that Japan created the first economic "miracle" in East Asia from the ashes of the war. From the early 1950s until the beginning of the 1990s, Japan's GNP grew at rates double those of most other members of the Organization for Economic Cooperation and Development (OECD), its share of world exports quadrupled, and its economy leapfrogged from the twentieth largest in the world to the second. Amazed by its rapid growth, renowned Harvard scholar Ezra Vogel called Japan the "number one" country in the world at the end of the 1970s.[1] Yet the Japanese economy experienced stagnation during the so-called lost decade of the 1990s before it was able to slowly recover. What explains Japan's impressive postwar economic growth, its setbacks, and its resurgence? Does the country's poor economic performance during the 1990s, including the years following the 1997 Asian financial crisis, spell the end of the Japanese "miracle"? Factors in Japan's economic development—including effective national policies such as the *Yoshida Doctrine* and the 1947 land reform, U.S. economic aid and military support, the Korean War, and the country's postwar cohesion, culture, and relationships with the international community—must all be addressed if we are to understand Japan's postwar development path.

THE YOSHIDA DOCTRINE AND THE 1955 SYSTEM

Postwar Japan was unhappy with its path towards militarism and war in the 1930s and chose to pursue a completely different course. In rebuilding Japan's major cities, which were destroyed by the air raids, several visions for Japan's future and its political outlook were proposed. Three most important ones were: social democracy, traditional nation-state, and "economics first."

Socialists opposed abolishing Article 9 of the postwar constitution and heavy reliance on the United States for

Japan's first postwar Prime Minister, Yoshida Shigeru.

7

security. At the forefront of these efforts was the Socialist Party which called for "unarmed neutrality" in diplomacy and security policy, opposing both the Japan-U.S. Security Treaty and the Self-Defense Forces (SDF). Seeing the future of "socialism" as just around the corner after "peace" and "democracy", this group opposed the conservatives and exerted a large influence in Japanese politics until around 1960. Influential postwar politicians Hatoyama Ichiro and Kishi Nobusuke and others advocated the traditional nation-state approach. They believed that postwar Japan, as a sovereign state, should have the military strength to deal with external threats and they called for constitutional revision and rearmament. The "normal country" discourse, heard after the 1990s, had its origin in the traditional nation-state approach in the early postwar period. The "economics first" line sought to rebuild postwar Japan as an economic and trading power through industrial development and international trade. It remade Japan into a pro-American state belonging to the Western camp in international politics and fostered a liberal democracy at home. Japanese politics in the postwar years developed through the intersection of these three political streams, although the "economics first" approach led by Yoshida Shigeru (1878–1967) became the dominant policy.[2]

The *Yoshida Doctrine* refers to the reconstruction policy devised by Yoshida Shigeru, Japan's first postwar Prime Minister. Yoshida served as Prime Minister from 1946 to 1947 and again from 1948 to 1954. The *Yoshida Doctrine* advocated adopting the U.S. stance on security and international relations issues and relying on U.S. military protection in order to allow Japan to focus its resources on economic production and the creation of a skilled labor force. Yoshida's aim was to focus all available resources on Japan's economic recovery while leaving its defense to the United States military. Japan would not spend more than 1 percent of its gross domestic product (GDP) on the military. In fact, attempts by the United States to persuade Japan to increase its military expenditures were rejected by Yoshida on the basis of the country's pacifist postwar constitution, in particular Article 9, under which Japan "renounces war as a sovereign right of the nation and the threat or use of force as means of settling international disputes." Yoshida's policies were greatly elaborated by his successors over the next several decades into a full-blown national strategy, and the *Yoshida Doctrine* served as the basic tenet of Japanese foreign policy in the postwar years through the Cold War.

While the *Yoshida Doctrine* set the tone for Japan's postwar reconstruction, the Korean War (1950–53) proved to be an unexpected shot in the arm and made it possible for Japan to make a fast economic recovery almost at a single stroke. The economic boom resulting from the Korean War was triggered by special procurements earnings from U.S. military expenditures and by the sudden rise in exports that accompanied the expansion of world trade after June 1950.

The term *1955 system* refers to the continuous dominance of the Liberal Democratic Party (LDP) over the Japanese political economy since 1955. Founded by different conservative factions in 1953, the LDP were overseers of Japan's economic development after the nation regained its sovereignty from the Allied (principally American) Forces in 1952. Whereas the LDP shared the neo-mercantilist view that Japan should become a competitive economic power, the party had to manage at least two different problems. Big businesses, elite bureaucrats, and politicians wanted to create large, internationally competitive firms through favorable industrial policies and fiscal responsibility but another key party constituency, small businesses and farmers, preferred local protection and subsidies. The LDP managed to reconcile these two competing interest groups by adopting an industrial policy of upgrading technologies and penetrating foreign markets while protecting the home turf from foreign competition.[3] With a secure domestic base, Japanese firms enjoyed a comparative advantage over foreign competitors.

The LDP's strength was based on an enduring coalition of business, agriculture, professional groups, and other interests. Elite bureaucrats collaborated closely with the party and interest groups in drafting and implementing economic policies. The system functioned efficiently as a locus for matching interest group money and votes with bureaucratic power and expertise. This arrangement resulted in problems such as corruption, but the party could claim credit for helping to create economic growth and a stable, middle-class Japan.

The *1955 system* ensured the continuity of Japanese economic and foreign policies from the 1950s until the early 1990s. In the August 1993 election of the Diet, the Japanese parliament, the LDP lost as a result of Japan's economic decline, scandals associated with party leaders, the lack of long-awaited reform programs, and factional rivalries within the party. The downfall of the LDP after thirty-eight years of rule is referred to as the "collapse of the *1955 system* or 1955 setup" in Japanese political history.

In 1994, the Japan Socialist Party and New Party Sakigake left the ruling coalition and joined the LDP in the opposition. With the help of the Socialist Party and New Party, the LDP was returned to power, although it allowed a Socialist to occupy the Prime Minister's chair. By 1996, the

LDP was able to return to power as a majority party. It was practically unopposed until 1998, when the opposition Democratic Party of Japan (DPJ) was formed. Since then, the opposition has gained momentum, especially in the 2003 and 2004 parliamentary elections.

In the July 2007 House of Councilors (the upper house of the Diet) elections, the LDP suffered a huge defeat and lost its majority for the first time in history while the DPJ managed to gain the largest margin in the upper house since its formation. The LDP was able to hold the majority in the House of Representatives (the lower house of the Diet) but had to share a coalition government with the conservative Buddhist New Komeito party. In the August 2009 general election, the DPJ defeated the LDP and Hatoyama Yukio became the first ever Prime Minister from the DPJ.

There was speculation after the 2009 election that Japan might develop into a two-party system. But the LDP was able to resume power after the December 2012 general election, ending the DPJ's brief control of the government. In the July 2013 House of Councilors election and the December 2014 House of Representatives election, the LDP-Komeito coalition secured the majority in both houses of the Diet (In September 2014 the LDP's junior partner New Komeito changed its name to Komeito), and the DPJ remained the largest opposition party. The Japanese Communist Party and the Innovation Party are two other major political parties in the mid-2010s. However, many Japanese have become fed up with politics. According to a survey by *Yomiuri Shimbun* in April 2010, almost half of Japanese voters did not support any political parties.

ZAIBATSU AND KEIRETSU

Zaibatsu and *keiretsu* played crucial roles in Japan's economic development and postwar reconstruction. *Zaibatsu* (財閥) refers to industrial and financial business conglomerates in the empire of Japan, whose influence and size allowed them to control significant parts of the Japanese economy from the Meiji period until the end of World War II. Very large *zaibatsu* such as the "Big Four" (Mitsubishi, Mitsui, Sumitomo, and Yasuda) were the most significant groups historically, having roots that stemmed from the Tokugawa period, 1603–1868.

After the Russo-Japanese War, a number of so-called second-tier *zaibatsu* emerged, mostly as the result of conglomeration and/or the winning of lucrative military contracts. Some of the more famous second-tier *zaibatsu* were the Okura, Furukawa, and Nakajima groups. All prospered in the boom years of World War II.

The American occupation dismantled the largest *zaibatsu* in the late 1940s, but the companies formed from the dismantling were soon reintegrated. The new corporations were linked through share purchases to form horizontally-integrated alliances across many industries. A *keiretsu* (系列, *system* or *series*) is a set of companies with interlocking business relationships and shareholdings. The prototypical *keiretsu* appeared in Japan following World War II. When possible, *keiretsu* companies would supply one another, making the alliances vertically integrated as well, assisted by a major bank in the group.

In addition to *keiretsu*, the Japanese economy during the postwar years was characterized by cooperation among manufacturers, suppliers, distributors, and banks; powerful enterprise unions; cozy relationships between businesses and government bureaucrats; and the guarantee of lifetime employment (*shushin koyo* 终身雇用) in big corporations and highly unionized blue-collar factories.

There are two types of *keiretsu*: vertical and horizontal. Vertical *keiretsu* illustrate the organization and relationships within a company (e.g., all factors in the production of a certain product are connected), while horizontal *keiretsu* illustrate relationships between member firms and industries, normally centered around a bank and trading company. Both are complexly woven together and help sustain each other.

A *keiretsu*'s bank lent money to the member companies and held equity positions in them. Each member bank had great control over the companies in the *keiretsu*, overseeing their activities and bailing them out if necessary. One effect of this was to minimize hostile takeovers in Japan because no single entity could challenge the power of the banks.

The close relationship between *zaibatsu*/*keiretsu* and the bureaucracy is another feature of Japan's economic policy, the so-called "developmental state" model. A recognized weakness of the closely knit relationship is its vulnerability to corruption and other economic scandals. Economic dominance and conservative research and development policies made it difficult for startups and new industries to emerge in the 1990s. Japan has a weak initial public offering (IPO) structure that considerably inhibits its growth potential. The IPO is the process of taking a privately owned company public by listing its shares on a stock exchange. A weak IPO process makes it difficult for companies to aggressively compete in cutting-edge technology markets because it is more difficult to raise investment start-up capital. Another weakness of this model is the fact that government bureaucrats often have a difficult time predicting the future.

Private sector entrepreneurs and corporate leaders helped enhance Japan's postwar economic growth and global competitiveness. For example, Honda Sōichirō (本田宗一郎), founder of the Honda Motor Company, Ltd., started his auto repair business in 1928 at the age of twenty-two. In 1948, he began producing motorcycles as president of the Honda Motor Company and turned the company into a billion-dollar multinational that produced the best-selling motorcycles in the world. In 1959, Honda went global and opened its first dealership in the United States. Toyoda Kiichiro (豊田喜一郎), founder of the Toyota Motor Corporation, made a strategic decision in 1937 to transform the Toyoda Loom Works, which he inherited from his father, into an automobile manufacturing facility, which was considered a risky business at the time. A few years after he died in 1952, his cousin, Toyoda Eiji, became head of the Toyota Motor Corporation, successfully expanded its business worldwide, and launched Japan's most prominent luxury vehicle brand, Lexus.

THE JAPANESE "MIRACLE"

Postwar inflation, unemployment, and shortages in all areas seemed overwhelming at first. Yet Japan experienced a phenomenal period of economic growth spurred partly by U.S. investment during the Korean War (1950–53) but mainly by the Japanese government's economic interventionism which often included providing incentives for private entrepreneurs, management, and labor to make high quality products. Some experts give full credit to Japan's Ministry of International Trade and Industry (MITI) for its role in the Japanese "miracle," although this claim remains controversial. The "miracle" continued to unfold during the "Golden Sixties." In 1965, Japan's nominal GNP was estimated at just over $91 billion. Fifteen years later it had soared to a record $1.065 trillion.

While the *Yoshida Doctrine* guided Japan's postwar economic and security policies, Prime Minister Ikeda Hayato (1960–64) has been described by some as the single most important figure in Japan's rapid growth during the 1960s. Under the leadership of Ikeda, a former minister of MITI, the Japanese government undertook an ambitious "income-doubling plan." Ikeda's plan predicted a 7.2 percent growth rate that would double the GNP over ten years, but by the second half of the 1960s average growth had climbed to an astounding 11.6 percent. Ikeda also actively promoted Japan's exports. In 1960, French president Charles De Gaulle famously referred to him as "that transistor salesman."[4] Ikeda furthered Japan's global economic integration by joining the General Agreement on Tariffs and Trade (GATT, the predecessor of the World Trade Organization

[WTO]) in 1963 and the International Monetary Fund (IMF) and OECD in 1964. Hosting the 1964 Summer Olympic Games reflected Japan's commitment to doubling GNP, as well as symbolizing its full reentry into the international community as a peaceful nation. By the time Ikeda left office, Japan's GNP was growing at a phenomenal rate of 13.9 percent annually. By the mid-1960s, 90 percent of Japanese households had their own televisions, refrigerators, and washing machines. In 1968 Japan became the second largest economy in the world, trailing only the U.S., a distinction it held until 2010 when China surpassed Japan.

Prime Minister Ikeda Hayato was credited with Japan's rapid growth in the 1960s.

Japan has few natural resources; trade helps it earn the foreign exchange needed to purchase raw materials for its economy. Manufacturing, construction, distribution, real estate, services, and communications are Japan's major industries. Today agriculture makes up only about 2 percent of the GNP. The most important agricultural product is rice. Japan's main export goods are cars, electronic devices, and computers. Its most important trading partner has traditionally been the United States, which still imports about one-fifth of all Japanese exports. However, since the mid-2000s China has been Japan's largest trading partner. The most important import goods are raw materials such as oil, foodstuffs, and wood.

The government played an effective leadership role in Japan's economic recovery. The Japanese "miracle" was achieved as a result of "guided capitalism" in which the state was heavily involved in economic activities and indeed provided official guidance in economic decision making to many businesses.

WHAT IS THE "DEVELOPMENTAL STATE" MODEL?

Since all states intervene in their economies, the question to pose is how and to what extent each government exercises its influence. *Developmental state* is a term used by international political economy scholars to refer to state-led macroeconomic planning in post-World War II East Asia. A developmental state intervenes directly in the economy through a variety of means to promote the growth of new industries and to reduce the dislocations caused by shifts in investment and profits from old to new industries. The developmental state model emphasizes the critical role of the state or government in promoting economic growth. Japan is considered the best example of such a state-guided economic system.

The concept of the developmental state was first articulated in Chalmers Johnson's 1982 book *MITI and the Japanese Miracle*, in which he recounted how MITI, the Ministry of International Trade and Industry, worked consistently and diligently to promote economic growth. This strong-state model of capitalism is vastly different from the liberal market system represented by the United States and Great Britain, where the state is supposed to stay away from market operations (laissez-faire) except in a regulatory capacity; it is also different from the purely state-dominated command economies of the former communist states. Johnson does not completely reject alternative explanations for the Japanese "miracle," but he decidedly gives the most weight to the role of the state and its industrial policies, declaring, "The significant difference is that in Japan the state's role in the economy is shared with the private sector, and both the public and private sectors have perfected means to make the market work for developmental goals" [5]. In the West, France has pursued a similar policy.

From its beginnings as the Ministry of Commerce and Industry (MCI) in 1925 to its transformation as the Ministry of Munitions (MM) in 1943, its reemergence as the MCI in 1945, and its reorganization as MITI in 1949, Japan's key economic bureaucracy has played a leading role in the nation's growth. In 2001, MITI's role was taken over by the newly created Ministry of Economy, Trade, and Industry (METI).

Established in 1949, MITI formalized cooperation between the Japanese government and private industry. It coordinated various industries, including the emerging *keiretsu*, toward the intersection of national production goals and private economic interests. It also boosted the industrial sector by untying the importation of technology from the importation of other goods. Realizing the importance of technology in development, MITI's Foreign Capital Law, passed in 1950, granted it the power to negotiate the prices and conditions of technology importation. This allowed it to promote industries MITI deemed promising. Productivity was greatly improved through new equipment, management, and standardization.

With the abolition of the Economic Stabilization Board and the Foreign Exchange Control Board in August 1952, MITI gained the ability to regulate imports. Its establishment of the Japan Development Bank in 1951 also provided the private sector with low-cost capital for long-term growth. The bank provided access to the Fiscal Investment and Loan Plan (FILP), a massive pooling of individual postal and national savings accounts. At the time, FILP controlled four times the savings of the world's largest commercial bank. FILP allowed the Japanese government to invest in infrastructure and public services without raising taxes.

Market forces alone could not produce the levels of growth Japanese leaders desired. While MITI might be an economic bureaucracy, it was not a bureaucracy of economists. In fact, many of its officials held law or public administration degrees from Japan's top universities.

The Japanese attempted to perfect the government-business relationship and employed it in more sectors than other capitalist nations. Japan's postwar political system has often been characterized as an "iron triangle" of conservative LDP politicians, big businesses, and elite bureaucrats. Japan's developmental state model has utilized elements from both the market and command economies to its advantage. Its state-guided economy demonstrates that a national government can use broad policy control over the economy to offset the disadvantage of late industrialization without the loss of private initiatives and incentives. An aggressive policy of government control over resource allocations for sectors such as agriculture and energy can accomplish a great deal in the early stages of economic development.

Johnson may have exaggerated the role of MITI while ignoring those of other ministries, especially the Ministry of Finance (MOF). In addition, the Japanese government was more democratic than Johnson described. Like other ministries, MITI was not dictatorial but responded to public demand. The important role of the state in Japan's postwar economic development was also studied by other scholars such as T. J. Pempel, Richard Katz, and Meredith Woo-Cumings.[6]

After the 1997 Asian financial crisis, the strong state model became associated with crony capitalism in many people's minds. *Crony capitalism* is a pejorative term for an allegedly capitalist economy in which success in business depends on close relationships between business people and government officials. It is typified by favoritism in the distribution of legal contracts, government grants, special tax breaks, and other favors government can bestow on particular businesses. However, some scholars think that Japan's development in the 1990s was actually a departure from the original "developmental state" model.

The International Environment and U.S. Aid

Any explanation of postwar Japan's economic development would be incomplete without a mention of the role of the United States. The post–World War II world was immediately plunged into the Cold War between Western governments, many of which were democratic, their allies, and communist governments. During the occupation, the United States successfully demilitarized and democratized Japan, turning it into a key ally in Asia. The American government, under the auspices of General Douglas MacArthur, Supreme Commander of the Allied Powers (SCAP), played a crucial role in Japan's initial economic recovery.

The 1950s stands out as a distinctive era in U.S.-Japan relations. In 1950, the two countries began negotiations to end the state of war between them. In these negotiations, the U.S. government also desired a Japanese commitment to the American side in the Cold War while the Japanese government sought an American guarantee of Japan's external defense. The result was the conclusion of two treaties in 1951 (which entered into force the following year): the multilateral San Francisco Peace Treaty, which brought the occupation to a close; and the bilateral U.S.-Japan Security Treaty, in which the United States pledged to maintain its military forces in and around Japan.

Following World War II, the United States provided reconstruction assistance to Japan. According to a study by the Congressional Research Service, total U.S. assistance to Japan in 1946–52 was roughly $15.2 billion in constant 2005 dollars, of which 77 percent was in the form of grants and 23 percent in loans. However, American aid to Japan was about half of what it provided for Germany, which totaled $29.3 billion in constant 2005 dollars from 1946 to 1952.[7]

Almost a third of U.S. assistance went to categories that would contribute directly to Japan's economic recovery (industrial materials, including machinery and raw goods; petroleum and petroleum products; and transportation, vehicles, and equipment). Most of the rest went for agricultural equipment, foodstuffs, and food supplies with smaller amounts spent on medical and sanitary supplies, education, and clothing.

The United States also provided technical help to Japan. In 1948 Joseph Dodge, Chairman of the Detroit Bank, went to Japan as an economic adviser to develop an austerity program for Japan. Through the "Dodge Plan", Japan tackled hyperinflation and was able to achieve a balanced budget by reducing government expenditures and by cutting back the size

General Douglas MacArthur and Emperor Hirohito, at their first meeting, at the U.S. Embassy, Tokyo, September 27, 1945. The American government, under the auspices of General MacArthur, Supreme Commander of the Allied Powers (SCAP), played a crucial role in Japan's initial economic recovery. Photo by U.S. Army photographer Lt. Gaetano Faillace.

of the bureaucracy. The United States had tense relations with both the Soviet Union and the People's Republic of China for most of the Cold War, which made Japan strategically very important to the United States. The United States and Western European economies also transferred industrial know-how to Japan, including DuPont's nylon patent, Bell Laboratory's transistor technology, and Corning's TV glass tube technology. A secure international environment protected by the United States and generous economic assistance helped facilitate Japan's economic takeoff in the postwar years.

Hostilities on the Korean Peninsula further boosted Japan's economy in 1950 because the United States paid the Japanese government large sums for special military procurements. These payments amounted to 27 percent of Japan's total exports that year. The Korean War brought a flood of American war orders, which temporarily alleviated Japan's chronic foreign trade imbalance. Prime Minister Yoshida famously called the

Korean War "a gift from the gods" for Japan. By 1953 when the Korean War armistice was signed, Japanese industrial production was almost restored to prewar levels. During the Korean War, SCAP departed and full sovereignty was returned to the government of Japan, except for Okinawa, which was returned to Japanese control in 1972. By the late 1960s, the United States had been absorbing one-third of Japan's total exports, becoming Japan's most important trading partner. The United States also insisted, over British opposition, that Japan be admitted to the GATT as a "temporary member." American sponsorship of Japan's admission to important international economic organizations, the United States' decision to allow Japan access to its market without demanding commensurate access to Japan's market for U.S. goods, and Japan's easy access to U.S. technology were all helpful during reconstruction.

THE JAPANESE BUBBLE AND THE FINANCIAL CRISIS

The state-guided, export-led strategy, despite some setbacks, worked well for Japan until the mid-1980s when the yen began to appreciate sharply after the 1985 Plaza Accord.[8] The Japanese currency went from 240 yen per U.S. dollar in 1985 to 150 in 1986 and 120 in 1988, doubling its value in three years, which severely crippled Japan's exports. Between 1986 and 1990, Japan experienced one of the greatest bubble economies in history. It began after the Japanese agreed to demands by other major industrialized nations that they substantially increase the value of the yen in 1985 (it doubled by 1988). When the Ministry of Finance lowered the prime interest rate from 5 percent to a postwar low of 2.5 percent, asset markets predictably skyrocketed. The value of commercially zoned property in central Tokyo, already the most expensive real estate in the world, jumped tenfold by 1989.

The Plaza Accord was meant to reduce Japan's mounting trade surpluses with the United States and other major economies, but the Japanese Ministry of Finance response of lowering interest rates and pressuring banks to issue widespread loans to stimulate the economy led to a huge bubble in real estate and stock values as buyers bid up asset prices. When the bubble burst in 1991 as a result of the MOF raising interest rates because of a fear of inflation, it ushered in a "lost decade" of economic stagnation during which Japan also suffered from the Asian financial crisis in 1997.

The financial crisis gripped much of Asia beginning in the summer of 1997. It started in Thailand where the government decided to float the baht, the Thai currency, and cut its peg to the U.S. dollar after exhaustive efforts to support it in the face of a severe financial overextension partly caused by a real estate bubble. As the crisis spread, most of Southeast Asia and Japan saw slumping currencies, devalued stock and other asset prices, and a precipitous rise in private debt. The Japanese economy did not collapse, but it was severely hit. Japan's GNP real growth rate slowed dramatically in 1997, from 5 to 1.6 percent, and sank to recession levels in 1998 due to intense competition from rivals. The unemployment rate reached a record 3.9 percent during the crisis.

The Asian financial crisis also led to more bankruptcies in Japan. In November 1997, Sanyo Securities and Yamaichi Securities (two of Japan's largest brokerages) and Hokkaido Takushoku (its tenth-largest bank) collapsed; shortly afterward Tokyo City Bank, a large regional bank, closed. The U.S. treasury secretary, Robert Rubin, urged Japan to shore up its banking system. In December 1997, Japan announced a series of reflationary measures, including a cut in the income tax. In January 1998, the Diet approved a $228 billion financial stabilization plan. In June 1998, the yen fell to an eight-year low against the U.S. dollar, driving down prices of stocks and currencies around the world. In September 1998, Japan Leasing Corp., a major leasing company, filed for bankruptcy protection. With a debt totaling $16 billion, it was then the largest bankruptcy filing since World War II.

THE JAPANESE ECONOMY IN THE TWENTY-FIRST CENTURY

In the 1970s and 1980s, Japan was the "next big thing." With a huge foreign exchange reserve, it adopted an investment-led strategy and began to purchase overseas, including capturing such iconic properties as the Rockefeller Center in New York. The United States was allegedly weakening in the wake of "the Rising Sun." Harvard professor Ezra Vogel in his 1979 book, *Japan as Number One*, analyzed traits that he thought contributed to the Japanese "miracle" such as basic education, low crime rates, a powerful but efficient bureaucracy, and a functioning democracy. Vogel was drawing lessons for America, hoping that it could do better and could respond constructively to the challenges from Japan. By the time his long-awaited 2001 sequel—*Is Japan Still Number One?*—was published, Japan had fallen to number twenty-one in the global growth competitiveness index ranking, according to the *World Competitiveness Yearbook* published by the Swiss International Institute for Management Development (IMD).[9] Vogel took up the issue of Japan's lost decade of the 1990s by attributing it to the very system he once praised. He provided lessons for Japan and suggested that it "needs a third wave of reforms as forward-thinking and as comprehensive as the reforms instituted in the Meiji era and during the early postwar era."[10]

What exactly happened to Japan's development model? What is the current status of the Japanese economy? Close government-industry cooperation, a strong work ethic, and mastery of high technology continue to help Japan advance with extraordinary speed and maintain one of the largest economies in the world today. Its reservoir of industrial leadership and technicians; a well-educated and industrious workforce; relatively high, albeit declining, savings and investment rates; and intensive promotion of industrial development and foreign trade have produced a mature industrial economy.

Japan's overall real economic growth from the 1960s to the 1980s has been called a "miracle": a 10 percent average in the 1960s, a 5 percent average in the 1970s, and a 4 percent average in the 1980s. Growth slowed markedly in the 1990s with an average growth rate of only 1 percent, largely due to the Bank of Japan's failure to cut interest rates quickly enough to counter the aftereffects of overinvestment during the late 1980s. Economic stagnation prolonged into the twenty-first century, causing some to call the 2000s the second "lost decade" of Japan. Japan is facing many challenges now. It is losing ground to aggressive Asian rivals, and desperately needs financial and structural reforms.

When Koizumi Junichiro was the prime minister from 2001 to 2006, he introduced some structural reforms in Japan including efforts to privatize the Japan Post. His six successors from 2006 to 2012 only stayed in office for about a year each, making it difficult to implement any meaningful economic and social policies. When Abe Shinzo, who succeeded Koizumi in 2006 and stayed in office for 11 months, became the prime minister again in December 2012, he introduced a series of economic policies to revive Japan's economy. Popularly called "Abenomics", his policies were based upon "three arrows": a bold, expansionary monetary easing by doubling the monetary base and depreciating the yen; a flexible fiscal policy that increased spending cuts and raised taxes; and a new growth strategy that enhanced competitiveness through structural reforms. With declining unemployment and improving domestic growth, the Japanese economy recovered at a slow rate under the leadership of Prime Minister Abe. Critics say that Prime Minister has put too much emphasis on security issues such as forcing a national security bill through the Diet in

Japan Today—Tokyo with Mount Fuji in the background.

2015, unnecessarily creating political divisions in Japanese society at a time when Japan really should focus on economic growth. Despite tense political relations between Japan and China, millions of Chinese tourists visit Japan every year, which contributes to Japan's economic rebound.

Japan provides the first example of an economy facing the challenge of producing growth in a society with a decreasing and aging population. The Japanese population peaked in 2005 and has been declining ever since. Studies suggest that the percentage of Japanese aged sixty-five and over will rise to 27.8 percent by 2020 and 29.6 percent by 2030. Meanwhile, in 2005, the age cohort zero to four years old (which will be the twenty- to twenty-four-year-old group in 2025) was 25 percent smaller than the current cohort of the same age.[11]

Exports have been a key driver of Japan's moderate recovery since the late 1990s, but in 2008 they fell for the first time in five years as a result of declining consumer demand in the United States and other countries as well as strong competition from developing economies, especially China and India. Meanwhile, due to rising oil prices, Japan's imports grew faster than exports and the trade surplus experienced its largest decline since 2001. In 2011, Japan recorded its first annual trade deficit in decades.

An aging and declining population presents one of the most serious challenges for Japan in the 21st century.

The 2008 global financial crisis and the 2011 triple disasters (earthquake, tsunami and nuclear plant meltdown) posed further challenges to Japan's recovery.

Japan remained the world's third largest economy in the 2010s and its foreign currency reserve the second largest in the world after China. The Japanese economy is moving in the direction of greater reliance on market forces and less on government guidance. However, global slowdown and a decline in inventories led to another recession in Japan at the end of 2015, highlighting serious challenges for Japan's full recovery.

The Japanese society is beginning to grapple with the implications of its political, economic, and demographic challenges. Issues such as whether more foreign workers should be allowed in and how the role of women in the labor force can be enhanced to increase productivity in a traditionally xenophobic and male-dominated society are seriously debated. As Tokyo gears up for the 2020 summer Olympics, the Japanese government and public hope that the international sporting event will help reenergize Japan and revive Japan's economy. Japan's participation in the US-led Trans-Pacific Partnership (TPP) may also help Japan's trade and economic growth.

3

SOUTH KOREA: FROM A COLONY
TO AN ECONOMIC POWER

The Korean Peninsula was traditional, feudal, agrarian, and isolated from the West until the late nineteenth century. Nicknamed "a shrimp among whales," Korea had always lived in the shadow of great powers. For much of its history, it was essentially a tributary state of imperial China.

The peninsula was a Japanese colony between 1910 and 1945, which brought both exploitation and modernization. Memories of the harsh colonial rule and different interpretations of history remain a key source of tensions in Japan-Korea relations today. Shortly after Japan surrendered, ending the Pacific War, on August 15, 1945, the peninsula was divided into North and South Korea. The United States took control south of the 38th Parallel while the Soviet Union took control of the north. The United Nations called for general elections on the peninsula in 1947, but the North Koreans refused. The Republic of Korea (ROK) was established in the south, and a communist form of government was adopted in the north (officially the Democratic People's Republic of Korea [DPRK]) in 1948. During the 1950–53 Korean War, the two Koreas, each supported by its great power allies, fought a bloody war. An armistice, but not a peace treaty, was signed in 1953—so technically the two Koreas are still at war.

South Korea began with an autocratic government, experimented with limited democracy in 1960–61, took an authoritarian turn in the 1960s, saw increased repression in the 1970s, and began genuine democratization in the late 1980s. With astonishing economic development from the 1960s to the 1980s, South Korea became one of the "Asian tigers." Since the late 1980s, it has also been one of the most vibrant democracies in the world. In 1996 it became the second country is Asia (after Japan) to be admitted to the Organization of Economic Cooperation and Development (OECD), a milestone in its development history.

A brief comparison between the two Koreas is contextually useful. The Republic of Korea (South Korea) was established on August 15, 1948, and headed by Syngman Rhee, a Princeton-educated, pro-Western, nationalist leader. The Democratic People's Republic of Korea (North Korea) was founded on September 9, 1948, under Kim Il-sung, who ruled the communist state until he died in July 1994. In 2015, South Korea had a population of about 49 million compared to North Korea's 24 million. Over a million Korean soldiers remain deployed against each other along the world's most heavily fortified border that separates the North and the South.

The DPRK originally had a larger industrial base than the ROK. It a socialist economy now, with the means of production largely in the hands of the government. Kim Il-sung's son Kim Jong-il ruled North Korea from 1994 until his death in 2011. While the country still largely follows the policy of *juche* (self-reliance), Kim Jong-il seemed more interested in modernizing his country and seeking diplomatic relations with the United States and Japan. He proposed a new development strategy of building *kangsong taeguk* (強盛大国 a strong and prosperous great state), which was similar to the Japanese objective before World War II and to the declared objectives of South Korean leader Park Chung-hee in the 1970s. Japan had adopted the strategy of *fukoku kyohei* (富国強兵 enriching the country, strengthening the military) when the Meiji Restoration began in 1868.

Kim Jong-il, leader of North Korea (1994–2011).

In the famines of the 1990s, two to three million North Koreans reportedly starved to death and the country was forced to turn to the international community for food and fuel. Instead of reforms, North Korea had chosen a *"songun"* (military first) strategy in the past few decades. The younger Kim also resorted to nuclear blackmail, which led to increased international pressure on the North's economy. The Six-Party talks (China, the United States, Russia, Japan, and the two Koreas are participants) that started in 2003 aimed to terminate North

Korean women and children search the rubble of Seoul for anything that can be used or burned as fuel. November 1, 1950. Capt. F. L. Scheiber. (Army)

Korea's nuclear program but stalled in 2009, and the nuclear issue remains a major obstacle in relations between North Korea and the United States and Japan.

After touring China and seeing the fruits of its economic reforms, Kim Jong-il initiated some reform measures in 2002. The Rajin-Sŏnbong Special Economic Zone was set up in the mid-1990s to attract foreign direct investment (FDI), much like the special economic zones (SEZs) in the PRC. The Rajin-Sŏnbong region was split from North Hamgyŏng Province in 1993 under the name "Rajin-Sŏnbong" (shortened to "Rasŏn" 罗先 in 2000). Joint ventures with the South were established in the Kaesong Industrial Park inside North Korea. Companies such as Unification of Korean Technologies (UNIKOTECH), a joint venture to develop and produce a simultaneous translation system over mobile phones, was set up in 2000. A North-South joint automobile firm, Peace Motors, was also established in 2000. In 1998, the Mount Kumgang tourism project was launched to enable South Koreans to cross the border and visit the North.

The Kim dynasty continued when Kim Jong-un who was under 30 years old succeeded his father Kim Jong-il in December 2011. Kim Jong-un introduced limited reforms and followed the "*byungjin*" policy (parallel

Kim Jong-un inspecting North Korean troops. Kim succeeded his father in 2011.

lines) of nuclear development and economic growth. Different from his grandfather and father who established warm ties with North Korea's key political and trading partner China, his relationship with China remained strained several years after he took office. By 2015 Chinese President Xi Jinping and South Korean President Park Geun-hye had met several times and visited each other's capitals, but Kim had not met with either Xi or Park.

Unlike the North, South Korea lacks natural resources. The small infrastructural base built during Japanese rule was mostly destroyed during the Korean War. As late as the early 1960s, very few people in the world thought South Korea could pull itself out of poverty. Per capita income in the early 1960s was even lower than those of Haiti, Ethiopia, and Yemen and about 40 percent below India's.[1] Unemployment and poverty were widespread with over 40 percent of the nation's population suffering from absolute poverty. Given these circumstances, South Korea's "rags to riches" story is not just fascinating but seemingly miraculous.

For most of the 1960s until the late twentieth century, South Korea enjoyed exponential economic growth, with one of the fastest growth rates in modern world history. The nation's GDP per capita grew from only $100 in 1963 to a record-breaking $10,000 in 1995 and reached $31,700 in 2011 and $35,300 in 2014. This phenomenon has been referred to as the "miracle on the Han River." Running through the capital city of Seoul, the Han River and its surrounding area has played a significant role in Korean history and economic growth. In comparison, North Korea's GDP per capita in 2013 was about $1,800.

The post–Korean War development strategy in South Korea can be divided into three phases: import substitution (1954–60), export orientation (1961–79), and balance and stabilization (post-1980). Import substitution industrialization is a trade and economic policy based on the premise that a country can reduce its foreign dependence through the local production of industrialized products. It was adopted by many Latin American countries from the 1930s to the late 1980s and by some Asian and African countries beginning in the 1950s. Import substitution policies in the wake of the Korean War resulted in lackluster growth performance, with an average real annual growth rate of 3.4 percent between 1953 and 1960. This period, however, was devoted to building the physical and human capital infrastructure that served as the basis for subsequent industrial development.

Park Chung-hee, South Korean leader from 1961 to 1979, was credited with South Korea's economic growth in the 1960s and 1970s, but he was also criticized for his authoritarian rule.

The second phase, export-oriented industrialization, began with President Park Chung-hee's military regime in 1961. Central to the strategy in this phase was the production of labor-intensive, light consumer goods for export, guided by centralized economic policy planning and implementation. For the next twenty years, the state-guided, export-based strategy of industrialization worked successfully. Export-oriented industrialization aims to speed up the industrialization process in a country through exporting goods for which the nation has a comparative advantage. Exports were identified as the "engine of growth" during this period. President Park's government normalized diplomatic relations with Japan in 1965, after which Japan provided over $800 million of financial support in the form of public and commercial loans and grants. South Korea's major ally the United States was willing to grant South Korea access to its market. In 1967, South Korea became a GATT contracting member and its exports were accorded most-favored-nation status in the global trading system. The success of the "Asian tigers"—Hong Kong, South Korea, Taiwan, and Singapore—in the post–World War II period is often credited to this export strategy. Between 1962 and 1979, South Korea's real GNP and exports grew at average annual rates of 9.3 and 33.7 percent, respectively. Leading ROK exports included electronics, textiles and footwear, automobiles and automobile parts, shipbuilding materials, and chemicals.

By the end of the 1970s, however, the Korean economy had overextended itself, and structural imbalances and bottlenecks were beginning to manifest themselves. The high growth rate led to a rapid

Syngman Rhee, the first president of South Korea after it was founded in 1948, led his country through the Korean War.

buildup of foreign debt and inflation, with widening disparities within industry as well as between rural and urban areas. The assassination of President Park in 1979, the oil-induced worldwide economic recession in 1980–81, and domestic crop failures compelled the new government to impose stabilization programs. The government started removing subsidies and preferential loans and called for an efficient allocation of investment to allow domestic industries to develop more in line with the shifting comparative advantages in the global market. In the aftermath of democratic transition, political, economic, and social dynamics unleashed by the process shaped the balance of power between the state and society. The government had to co-opt and accommodate various social forces to stabilize the economy and politics.

South Korea also participated militarily in the Vietnam War in the late 1960s and the early 1970s and provided war-related supplies to the American troops, resulting in substantial foreign exchange earnings. South Korea's industrialization did not take place at the expense of other sectors, notably agriculture. There were periods, particularly the early 1970s, when agriculture assumed a critical role in development strategy, and the South Korean government was able to avoid an excessive urban-rural income disparity. The ROK government launched the *Saemaul Undong* (the New Community or New Village Movement) in 1970 to improve rural infrastructure and raise rural income. The initiative helped reduce the urban-rural gap and broadened the base of development and shared growth. The government did not have to spend a large percentage of its budget on social welfare and could concentrate its limited resources on high-growth sectors of the economy. The *Saemaul Undong* was hailed as a great success in the 1970s but lost its momentum during the 1980s as economic and political environments in South Korea changed rapidly. As a result of the 1997 Asian financial crisis, output in South Korea fell almost 7 percent, while a record number of 1.2 million Koreans were out of job. The 1999 National Basic Livelihood Security Act, which set minimum standards of living as a universal right, elevated the level of

South Korean social welfare a step further by providing a cash benefit and in-kind support such as health care and education to eligible people living in absolute poverty.

CHAEBOL

The *chaebol*, a form of business conglomerate, is the symbol of South Korea's economic success. Several dozen such large, family-controlled, government-assisted corporate groups have played a major role in the South Korean economy since the 1960s. Some have become well-known international brand names such as Samsung, Hyundai, Daewoo, SK, and LG. The *chaebols* are powerful independent actors in the economy and politics, and they cooperate with the government in planning and innovation. The government has worked hard to encourage competition among them in industries such as electronics and automobiles to avoid monopolies. *Chaebols* depended on a credit-based system of industrial finance. Nationalization of banks in the early 1960s allowed the government to have full control of credit lines to channel resources to strategic sectors and to encourage *chaebols* to invest in targeted areas such as electronics and automobiles.

Chaebols and their leaders helped pull the Korean economy out of poverty and eventually made it globally competitive. Lee Byung-Chul, founder of the Samsung Group, started a small trading company with forty employees in 1938. In 1953, he opened a sugar refinery, South Korea's first manufacturing facility after the Korean War. The company prospered under Lee's philosophy of making Samsung the leader in each industry he entered. After his initial success, he ventured into service businesses such as insurance, securities, and department stores in the 1960s and 1970s. South Korean President Park Chung-hee's regime helped Samsung and many other Korean firms. President Park placed great importance on economic growth and development, and he assisted large, profitable companies, protecting them from competition and aiding them financially as well. His government restricted several foreign companies such as Micron of the United States and Sharp of Japan that were selling consumer electronics in South Korea. Both companies were required to hand over advanced semiconductor technology in return for access to the Korean market. This helped Samsung enormously when it began to manufacture the first Korean dynamic random access memory chips. As it continued to thrive in the domestic market, Samsung invested heavily in research and development and began to go global in the late 1980s and early 1990s, turning the company into a worldwide leader in the electronics industry. In

Table 3.1. Chaebol and Keiretsu Compared

	Chaebol 财阀	*Keiretsu* 系列
History	Relatively short	Much longer
Management	Largely by founding families	Mostly by professional executives
Ownership	Centralized	More decentralized
Production Structure	Subsidiaries produce components for export products	External contractors are hired for production
Financial Structure	Subject to government regulation in credit allocation. Prohibited from owning private banks	Historically working with an affiliated bank with almost unlimited access to credit

1982, it built a television assembly plant in Portugal; in 1984, the company constructed a $25 million plant in New York; and in 1987 Samsung created another $25 million facility in England.

Chaebols are often compared to Japan's *keiretsu*, the successors to the prewar *zaibatsu* (in fact, *chaebol* and *zaibatsu* are Korean and Japanese pronunciations of the same Chinese characters, 财阀). While *chaebols* are similar to *keiretsu*, there are many differences between them (see Table 3.1).

DEMOCRACY AND DEVELOPMENT

South Korea's transformation from a poor, authoritarian state to a prosperous, democratic one raises an interesting question: can or should a country focus on economic modernization before political democratization? An important issue in international political economy is how economic development and political regimes interact. The political scientist Seymour Martin Lipset pointed out in the 1950s that a high level of economic development made democracy more likely. Another political scientist, Samuel Huntington, has observed that while developed countries tend to have stable democracies, the process of economic development may lead to political instability, which makes it likely and even desirable to have an authoritarian government during the transition period.[2] South Korea's experience supports both arguments.

After the "people power" movement of 1987 against the heavy-handed governance of President Chun Doo-hwan, the government agreed to a democratic transition based on a pact among elements of the military regime and the two major opposition parties. The 1987 new constitution provided for a democratically elected president limited to one five-year term. All three major political figures in 1987, Kim Yong-sam, Kim Dae-jung, and Roh Moo-hyun, held presidential office later on. Democracy has been fully consolidated in South Korea: the military is under civilian control, elections are vigorously contested, and the courts have become major sites for the constraint of politics.

Kim Dae-jung, the first leader from the South to cross the border to visit North Korea in 2000. Kim won the Nobel Peace Prize in 2000.

Lee Myung-bak, who became the ROK's seventeenth president in February 2008, was an executive and later president of Hyundai—one of the largest *chaebols*—before he entered politics in 1992. Nicknamed "the Bulldozer," Lee was a no-nonsense executive single-mindedly focused on growth. He later paid more attention to quality of life and the environment. In 2005, as mayor of Seoul, he restored a paved-over, four-mile stream in downtown Seoul over which an ugly highway had been built during the "growth at all cost" 1970s. Promising to improve the quality of life for Seoul residents, he had the traffic-clogged elevated highway ripped out and restored the Cheonggyecheon (literally, "clear water stream"), which had been covered over. The project propelled him into the international spotlight, and *Time* magazine named him one of its Heroes of the Environment in 2007.

President Lee wanted to be the chief executive officer of the nation. His stated goals were expressed in "the 747 plan" during his election campaign (a reference to the Boeing 747 aircraft): achieving 7 percent annual growth and $40,000 per capita GDP and making Korea the world's seventh-largest economy. He was not able to achieve those objectives when his term expired in 2013.

THE LIMITS OF THE "DEVELOPMENTAL STATE" MODEL

South Korea also followed the developmental state model, with active government guidance of economic activities. While this model has yielded

A Buddhist statue gazing at the cityscape of modern Seoul, capital of South Korea.

some good economic performances for East Asian economies, it has been blamed by some for the 1997 financial crisis. South Korea had been building great conglomerates to compete on the world stage. The *chaebol*, supported and sometimes controlled by government, absorbed more and more capital investment. Eventually, excess debt led to major failures and takeovers. The banking sector was burdened with nonperforming loans as large corporations were funding aggressive expansions. In July 1997, South Korea's third-largest car maker, Kia Motors, applied for emergency loans. In 1998, Hyundai took over Kia Motors. The Seoul stock exchange fell by 4 percent on November 7, 1997. On November 8, it plunged by 7 percent, its biggest one-day drop to date. The Korean won, meanwhile, weakened to more than seventeen hundred per dollar from around eight hundred. In the post-1997 financial crisis reform, the *chaebol* lost its ability and credibility to drive the reform agenda.

As a later developer than Japan, South Korean leaders' perception was the nation needed a stronger government to promote economic growth and the South Korean state was even more interventionist than the Japanese. The objective of fast industrialization and the effort to support large businesses were mutually reinforcing. The big South Korean *chaebols* such as Hyundai and Daewoo, which the government supported, did become internationally competitive. But cozy state-business relationships sometimes lead to corruption, and that is what happened in South Korea and Japan, hence the name "crony capitalism."[3]

On the other hand, if the state misallocates resources, as in the case of North Korea, where the military receives priority in the distribution of limited resources, economic growth will stagnate and ordinary citizens will remain in poverty.

The term *strong government* has been criticized as implying a compliant society, which is often not the case in East Asia. Even in South Korea, which is frequently recognized as having the strongest development state in East Asia, the society has sometimes been militantly opposed to the state.[4] The society's power *vis-à-vis* the state was typified by the Gwangju uprising. This popular uprising took place in the city of Gwangju in May 1980 when citizens rose up against Chun Doo-hwan's military dictatorship. The uprising was crushed by the South Korean military with hundreds of civilian casualties, but it helped to pave the way for South Korean democratization. Labor, farmer and civic groups have frequently rallied in Seoul and other cities to protest against the government's trade and other policies today.

A LEADER IN R&D AND GREEN ECONOMY

The South Korean economy's long-term challenges include a rapidly aging population, inflexible labor market, dominance of *chaebols*, and heavy reliance on exports. To address these challenges and sustain economic growth, the Park Geun-hye administration (2013-2018) prioritized structural reforms, deregulation, promotion of entrepreneurship and creative industries, and the competitiveness of small and medium enterprises. By 2015 South Korea had signed free trade agreements with major powers including the United States and China. In the mid-2010s South Korea's economy remained the fourth largest in Asia after China, Japan and India and the 14th largest in the world.

Park Geun-hye, ROK president (2013-2018), is the daughter of former president Park Chung-hee.

South Korea's average growth rate for the 1991–95 period was 7.5 percent, but it slipped to 4.6 percent in 2001–07. Its economy slowly rebounded after the crisis. In the 2010s, South Korea continued to emphasize innovation and focused on green technology as a way to upgrade its economy to become globally competitive. For example, the Roh Moo-hyun administration (2003-2008) created the five-year Basic Plan of Science and Technology and identified ten technologies as priorities such as biotechnology and green technology. The Lee Myung-bak government (2008-2013) promoted the Green Economy in the second five-year Basic Plan and chose "new growth engines" in green technology. The first woman to become President of South Korea, Park Geun-hye who assumed office in 2013, launched a new five-year Basic Plan to propose the Creative Economy, aimed to strengthen R&D ties to economic growth, technology commercialization and job creation. According to OECD, South Korea's R&D investment in 2012 was already the highest in OECD economies, with its gross domestic expenditure on R&D reaching 4.36 percent of its GDP, much higher than the 2.4 percent OECD average.

4

THE PRC AND TAIWAN: THE STORY OF A "DRAGON" AND A "TIGER"

China's phenomenal economic transformation and achievements since the late 1970s raise a few interesting questions. How does its development path differ from those of other East Asian economies? Is China moving toward democracy? And what are the main development challenges for China's future?

Modern Chinese history began with the so-called "century of humiliation." China suffered enormously as a result of clashes with the Western powers in the nineteenth century. The "century of humiliation" began in 1839 when the British used "gunboat diplomacy" to impose unfair trade practices on the Qing dynasty. When the Chinese resisted, the British started the first Opium War, which lasted from 1839 to 1842, weakened the Qing dynasty, and marked the beginning of the colonization and exploitation of China. France, the United States, Russia, Germany, and later Japan all took advantage of China's weakness to establish spheres of influence. They forced the Qing to sign treaties recognizing their zones of incursion. It was during this period that the British forced China to cede Hong Kong to them as a colony, and Japan took Taiwan as a colony after it defeated China in the first Sino-Japanese War (1894–95). After Chinese revolutionaries overthrew the Qing dynasty in 1911, the country suffered internal strife for nearly four decades due to warlordism, civil wars, and the Japanese invasion.

Revolutionaries such as Dr. Sun Yat-sen attempted to save China by introducing "Mr. Science" and "Mr. Democracy." Sun and his followers established the Republic of China (ROC) in 1911 after the Qing dynasty collapsed. The Republic's founding father proposed "Three Principles of the People" (*sanmin zhuyi* 三民主义)—the principle of *Minzu* (Nationalism), the principle of *Minquan* (People's Power), and the principle of *Minsheng* (People's Livelihood)—to save the beleaguered nation. Sun's "Three

Principles" were apparently inspired by "government of the people, by the people, and for the people," the phrase Abraham Lincoln used in the Gettysburg Address. Unfortunately, competition for power by warlords and Sun's death in 1925 dashed the hope for a democratic and wealthy China.

The Chinese Civil War of the 1940s eventually created "two Chinas." Chiang Kai-shek and his Nationalist forces were defeated on the mainland and retreated to Taiwan. The Republic of China (ROC) government, though beaten on the battlefield, was not destroyed; instead, it survived and prospered in Taiwan. On the mainland, Mao Zedong's Communist forces unified most of the country and established the People's Republic of China in October 1949. The "century of humiliation" ended with Mao's powerful declaration at Tiananmen Square that all foreign influences had been driven out of China and "the Chinese people have stood up." The two Chinese governments took different development paths. Today Taiwan, one of the four "little dragons," is free and prosperous and the PRC, after its opening up in the late 1970s, is quickly modernizing and building a market economy with Chinese characteristics.

The Chinese Communists made many social and political changes, starting in the 1950s with the transition to a planned economy. Mao also launched a series of political campaigns, including the "Great Leap Forward" (1958–61), during which he boasted that China would catch up with Great Britain and the United States in industrialization within fifteen years. As a result of this unrealistic, radical policy, although estimates of the number of deaths vary, most historians agree that about 25–30 million Chinese starved to death. Mao later orchestrated the "Cultural Revolution" (1966–76), during which young students ("Red Guards") were encouraged to "make revolution" and attack intellectuals and veteran party leaders. In this decade, colleges across China were closed and economic growth lagged even farther behind that of its thriving neighbors. In the first three decades of PRC history, the country had only limited trade with the Soviet Union and a few developing nations and was essentially isolated from the Western world and the global economy. Shortly after Mao's death in 1976, the Chinese government, under Deng Xiaoping's leadership, introduced economic reforms as well as limited political reforms and began to open itself to the West again.

THE TAIWANESE "MIRACLE"

When the ROC government recovered Taiwan from its Japanese colonizers in 1945, the island was in a state of widespread destruction. Railways, roads, and harbors were basically operating at half capacity. Outbound transportation was inconvenient and manufacturing productivity sharply reduced. Basic necessities were in short supply, and prices were continuously skyrocketing.

When Chiang Kai-shek and his Kuomintang (KMT) government fled to Taiwan in 1949 following the Chinese Civil War, they brought China's precious metals and foreign currency reserves to the island with them. Many mainland business and intellectual elites also escaped to Taiwan.

The KMT government took advantage of the still-functioning agricultural and industrial infra-structure built by the Japanese as well as what raw materials and food reserves remained on the island.

Chiang Kai-shek, a nationalist who strongly believed in "one China."

It also instituted several laws and land reforms that had never been effectively enacted on the mainland. Some of these reforms are briefly described later in this chapter.

Huge amounts of American aid also injected new blood into Taiwan's economic life. The United States provided short-term financial assistance, easy credit, and military support, which helped Taiwan raise the necessary capital to restart its economy. The United States then temporarily terminated aid to Taiwan after the PRC was established in 1949. After the Korean War broke out in 1950, the U.S. government resumed its economic aid and assisted in the defense of the Taiwan Strait as part of the Cold War. This not only boosted morale but also stabilized the island's economy.

The KMT government was determined to develop Taiwan into a solid base for its efforts to "recover" the lost Chinese mainland. Chiang Kai-shek initially hoped to return to the mainland but gradually accepted the fact that the ROC government was in Taiwan to stay. While maintaining its military preparedness, Taiwan quickly adopted land and other economic reforms.

Sun Yat-sen had made "land to the tiller" a foundation of the early Chinese republic, but the KMT never had sufficient control over China to implement any reforms. In the 1950s, Taiwan's land reform and community development plans were carried out by the Sino-American Joint Commission on Rural Reconstruction (JCRR). The JCRR was established in 1948, before the move to Taiwan, and funded by U.S. Congress based on a provision in the China Aid Act of 1948. It was led by five commissioners, three of whom were Chinese, appointed by the Chinese government, and the other two were Americans appointed by the U.S. President. In 1949, with the impending defeat of the KMT and its retreat to Taiwan, the JCRR moved to the island, where under the leadership of Chiang Monlin (Jiang Menglin) it supervised major land reforms, agricultural improvements, and education projects. The Columbia-educated Chiang had previously served as the President of Peking (Beijing) University and Zhejiang University and as Minister of Education under the ROC government.

Many of the large landowners in Taiwan were Japanese who had fled. Those who stayed were compensated with commercial and industrial properties seized after Taiwan reverted from Japanese rule in 1945. Starting in 1949, rents were reduced to 37.5 percent of the original and landlords were required to provide six-year leases. Tenants were no longer required to pay rent in advance, and during times of crop failure they could apply for a reduction. This had the immediate effect of lowering land prices and facilitating the process of land redistribution. The KMT government also sold public lands abandoned by the Japanese to farmers at a fixed rate. The farmer was loaned the money and could repay it in kind over ten years. Later, larger landowners were forced to sell their land, except for small amounts, on the same terms. The land program succeeded in part because the KMT had come from the mainland and had few ties to local landowners. Like the 1947 land reform in Japan, it created small independent farmers whose economic resources were enhanced by their new status.

To accomplish the central mission of economic growth, the Taiwanese government allowed technocrats rather than politicians to handle economic decision making. Since Taiwanese natives controlled the private sector, the government created state-owned enterprises to promote heavy industrialization. It was also easier for an outsider government without local ties to conduct these reforms, which not only benefited the economy but also benefited the KMT by weakening local power bases that might have posed a challenge to its rule. At the same time, the KMT allowed Taiwanese businesses to operate with few restrictions, limiting the scope of the state enterprises. There was thus plenty of room for social mobility and economic advancement.[1]

Individual businesses and corporate entrepreneurs played an essential role in helping make Taiwan one of the most dynamic and globally competitive economies in the world. One of them, Wang Yung-ching (also

A night view of Taipei with the Taipei 101 Tower. © Imaginechina.

known as Y.C. Wang 王永庆), founded a large business empire. He served as chairman of the board of the Formosa Plastics Corporation, one of the largest plastics manufacturers in the world, until June 2006, when he stepped down at the age of eighty-nine. He also chaired the boards of the Nan Ya Plastics Corporation, the Formosa Chemistry and Fibre Corporation, and the Cyma Plywood and Lumber Company. His businesses funded Taiwan's Ming-chi Institute of Technology, Chang Gung Memorial Hospital, and Chang Gung University. His global investments focused on the United States and mainland China. Several of his children followed in his footsteps and became well established in the semiconductor, computer, and other industries. Wang died in his sleep at age 91 in October 2008 during a visit to the U.S.

Prior to 1962, Taiwan's agricultural production contributed more to GDP than industrial production; in 1952, agriculture's share of GDP was 32.2 percent and that of industry 16.7 percent. However, in 1961 agriculture's share fell to just 25 percent, while the industrial sector's share rose to 23.7 percent. In 1962, the value of industrial production began to exceed that of agriculture, and scholars generally concur that this marks the beginning of post-war Taiwan's "industrial era." By 1986, industrial output had climbed to a full 47.1 percent of GDP. Between 1952 and 1982, economic growth averaged 8.7 percent, and GDP grew by 360 percent between 1965 and 1986. The period between 1963 and 1980 witnessed the most rapid growth in the history of Taiwan. Despite the adverse effects of two energy crises, it maintained an annual growth rate of 10 percent. The income gap between rich and poor declined during this period. The Gini coefficient—an internationally applied index that measures income inequality—was 0.558 in 1953 and fell to 0.303 in 1980, a score even lower than those of some Western European countries.[2] Health care, education, and quality of life also greatly improved during this period.

The Taiwanese government provided great opportunities for small and medium enterprises (SMEs) employing anywhere from two to 200 workers. SMEs specialized in shoes, clothing, toys, small appliances, and consumer electronics and were contract employees for Japanese and US firms which, because of high costs, had moved their operations to Taiwan. Many SMEs began relocating to Southeast Asia in the 1980s due to rising labor costs in Taiwan. At the end of 2010, SMEs still played a critical role in Taiwan's economy. They accounted for almost 98 percent of all enterprises and employed 8.19 million workers, about 78 percent of Taiwan's labor force, the highest percent of employment in this category of the four "little dragons."[3]

Taiwan's economy has been boosted by its robust exports, and as of 2015 it had the world's fifth-largest foreign exchange reserves after the PRC, Japan, Saudi Arabia, and Switzerland. It is the world's largest supplier of computer chips and a leading liquid crystal display (LCD) panel and networking equipment manufacturer and consumer electronics designer and manufacturer. Textile production is another major industrial export sector, although its importance has declined due to fierce competition from other economies.

THE UNITED STATES AND THE "TWO CHINAS"

Recognizing that Chiang Kai-shek could never defend Taiwan against Mao's powerful and still growing forces, the United States was prepared to abandon it in the late 1940s. To a great extent, the Korean War saved Taiwan. Shortly after the war broke out in June 1950, the United States sent its Seventh Fleet into the Taiwan Strait, forestalling an imminent PRC attack on the island. The signing of the US-ROC Mutual Defense Treaty in 1954 officially put Taiwan under U.S. military protection.

The Korean War turned the PRC and the United States, which had been exploring mutual diplomatic recognition, into enemies. Although official contacts continued in places such as Warsaw and Geneva, relations did not improve until President Richard Nixon's 1972 visit to China. A year earlier the United Nations had recognized the PRC rather than the ROC as

China's legitimate government. In 1973, the United States established a liaison office in Beijing, with George H. W. Bush serving as its head in 1974 and 1975. In 1979, the United States and the PRC finally established diplomatic relations and Washington cut its official ties with Taiwan. In a joint communiqué, the United States acknowledged that Taiwan was part of China and that the PRC was the sole government representing it.

Years later many in Taiwan still cannot forgive the United States for its "betrayal," and President Jimmy Carter, who normalized diplomatic ties with Beijing, is still verbally attacked by some politicians. However, it was President Carter who also signed the "Taiwan

Chiang Ching-kuo, Chiang Kai-shek's son, introduced democratic reforms in Taiwan in the 1980s.

Relations Act" (TRA) into law in April 1979, the statute that has regulated the U.S.-Taiwan unofficial relationship ever since. These relations are sometimes described as "officially unofficial and unofficially official." Although neither the PRC nor Taiwan is completely satisfied with the arrangement, many argue that the dual U.S. approach (i.e., officially recognizing the PRC while maintaining strong nongovernmental relations with Taiwan) serves the best interests of the United States. Under this framework, the United States has continued to provide weapons to Taiwan for defensive purposes and, perhaps most significantly, Taiwan has prospered and democratized.

Taiwan's democratization was gradual and peaceful. In the 1950s and 1960s, it suffered under the so-called white terror, during which over 140,000 people were jailed or executed for opposing KMT rule. In 1986, President Chiang Ching-kuo, Chiang Kai-shek's son, initiated democratic reforms by expanding political participation, and the opposition Democratic Progressive Party (DPP) was formed. Martial law, which had been imposed in May 1949, was finally lifted in July 1987. The younger Chiang was hoping that a democratic Taiwan would serve as a vanguard for democratizing mainland China. In Taiwan's first democratic presidential election in 1996, Lee Teng-hui, the KMT chairman but also an advocate of Taiwan independence, was elected to a four-year term. In 2000, the opposition DPP leader Chen Shui-bian won the presidential election in a peaceful transition of power. In 2004, Chen was reelected in a hotly contested race after he suffered two mysterious

Tsai Ing-wen from the DPP became the ROC's first woman president in 2016.

bullet wounds on election eve. The KMT and others allege that Chen staged the assassination attempt in order to win the sympathy vote, but Taiwan's Supreme Court dismissed this charge as well as others regarding election fraud. However, the incident is still controversial.

During the eight years of the DPP rule (2000–2008), Taiwan's economy and its international position were both weakened by global economic fluctuations and the PRC's negative opinion of President Chen. The number of countries that recognized Taiwan had dropped from thirty-one to twenty-three by 2008. President Chen repeatedly claimed that China and Taiwan were two separate countries on each side of the Taiwan Strait. People in Taiwan are experiencing an identity shift. The majority used to consider themselves as both Taiwanese and Chinese, but now most people identify themselves as Taiwanese only as a result of the Chen administration's de-sinicization education, a policy designed to deliberately cut Taiwan's links to China and make it a separate country. Cross-Strait relations were extremely tense during Chen's tenure, and Beijing adopted a strategy of waiting Chen out. Chen was arrested and indicted for forgery, money-laundering, and misuse of public funds at the end of 2008 and was sentenced to 19 years in prison, reduced from a life sentence. He was granted medical parole in January 2015. His supporters have insisted that his trial was unfair and politically motivated by the KMT.

After the victory of KMT leader Ma Ying-jeou in the March 2008 presidential election, Taiwan adopted a more moderate policy toward mainland China, and cross-Strait relations greatly improved. Mainland Chinese can now visit Taiwan and mainland and Taiwan students can study on each other's campuses. In December 2008, direct passenger flights, shipping, and postal services across the Taiwan Strait were reinstated for the first time in nearly six decades. At the end of 2015 there were 120 daily flights between the two sides. Many restrictions on Taiwanese investment on the mainland imposed by previous Taiwanese administrations were lifted. Taiwan and mainland China signed the landmark Economic Cooperation Framework Agreement (ECFA) in 2010. Ma was reelected in 2012. During

Ma's two terms, 23 economic, trade and other non-political agreements were signed between the PRC and Taiwan. In November 2015, Ma and Chinese president Xi Jinping held a historic meeting in Singapore, the first between leaders of the two governments after 1949. Avoiding using their official titles and insisting on equality, they called each other "Mr." and even split the dinner bill. As the DPP prepares to return to power after the 2016 elections, cross-Strait relations have entered a new period of uncertainty.

Closer economic ties between Taiwan and mainland China have not benefited everyone in Taiwan. With dwindling economic opportunities on the island and growing concerns about overreliance on the mainland economically and eventually politically, many in Taiwan, especially young people, became frustrated with the Ma government during his second term. In spring 2014, angry student protestors stormed into the Legislative Yuan and Executive Yuan and occupied the Legislative Yuan for 23 days, paralyzing the legislative body which was about to pass the goods and service trade agreement with the mainland. Nicknamed the "Sunflower Movement", the DPP-backed student protests led to heated debate in Taiwan about democracy, rule of law and cross-Strait relations.

THE CHINESE "MIRACLE"

On the mainland, Mao Zedong's often turbulent policies plunged China into deep social, economic, cultural, and political chaos, and in 1976, at the end of the Cultural Revolution, the Chinese economy was on the brink of collapse. Deng Xiaoping, the next significant PRC leader, initiated pragmatic and experimental policies that fundamentally changed the fate of China. His "cat theory," which claims that it doesn't matter whether a cat is white or black so long as it catches mice, established a climate that continues in which economic results, often achieved by capitalism, take precedence over rigid ideological adherence to socialism. Officially, beginning with Deng, the PRC has been building "socialism with Chinese characteristics." A closer look at China's policies and practices in the past three

Mao Zedong and his Communist forces defeated Chiang Kai-shek's Nationalists and founded the People's Republic of China in 1949. China under Mao was one of the poorest nations in the world.

Shenzhen city in south China's Guangdong province. After being designated as a Special Economic Zone in 1979, Shenzhen quickly transformed from a small fishing village into a large metropolis. Photo © Imaginechina.

decades suggests that the PRC has probably been building "capitalism with Chinese characteristics." Some suggest that China has adopted an economic system of state capitalism, although the political structure is still under the tight control of the Communist Party. Deng's vision notwithstanding, what other factors have helped propel China's economic growth? What is unique about China's experience? Can Taiwan, as a Chinese society, serve as a beacon for the mainland's continued pursuit of modernization and democracy?

China's reforms began in the late 1970s in the countryside, where Deng introduced the "household responsibility system," under which farmers could rent a piece of land from the state and sell their surplus crops on the open market. Rural entrepreneurs were also encouraged to establish their own businesses, called "township and village enterprises (TVEs)."

Meanwhile, China reopened trade with the West. At first, its strategy was *yin jin lai* (引进来), which means "to bring in" foreign direct investment. In 1979 the PRC established four special economic zones (SEZs) in southern China near Hong Kong, Taiwan, and Southeast Asia to attract direct investment from overseas Chinese and Western businesses. Investors enjoyed preferential treatment in taxation and exports. China was very cautious in this initiative since these were new reform policies. With the SEZ experiment, China was "crossing the river while groping for the stone," as Deng Xiaoping put it. The SEZs turned out to be a great success. For example, Shenzhen, the best-known SEZ, grew literally overnight from a small fishing village into a glitzy modern metropolis.

After the success of the SEZs, Deng opened up the whole coastal area, including Shanghai, in the late 1980s and early 1990s. In his famous 1992 "southern tour," he praised what the SEZs especially Shenzhen had achieved and urged the rest of China to "move faster and be bolder." He did not include Shanghai in the first wave of economic liberalization in the early 1980s, fearing that if the Shanghai experiment failed the whole nation's economy would suffer seriously since Shanghai alone accounted for one-sixth of the national GDP. Shanghai began to prosper later, in the early 1990s when its modern Pudong district emerged on the east side of the Huangpu River. In the twenty-first century, Shanghai remains China's economic and commercial center.

After over two decades of *yin jin lai*, China adopted a new strategy, *zou chu qu* (走出去) or "going out," in the late 1990s. Chinese companies began to invest abroad, just as Japanese companies had a couple of decades before. As an example of *zou chu qu*, in the summer of 2005 the China National Offshore Oil Company, Ltd. (CNOOC), attempted to purchase Unocal, a small California oil company, although the sale was aborted due to pressure from the U.S. Congress. China has invested heavily in Africa, Latin America, the Middle East, and Central Asia, especially in energy sectors. In November 2007, the Industrial and Commercial Bank of China announced that it would be purchasing a 20 percent stake in the Standard Bank of South Africa worth $5.6 billion. In October 2014 the Anbang Insurance Group of China purchased the landmark Waldorf Astoria in New York for $1.95 billion, making it the most expensive hotel ever sold. China agreed to build a nuclear power plant for the United Kingdom during President Xi's visit to London in October 2015. In early 2016 a Chinese company offered $43 billion to buy Swiss agrochemicals giant Syngenta. China also plans to invest in America's first high-speed rail line between Las Vegas and Los Angeles.

In 2015 the China-led Asian Infrastructure Investment Bank (AIIB) went operational, which gives China new venues for investment in developing nations. President Xi Jinping also unveiled the "One Belt, One Road" project in 2013. The land-based "Silk Road Economic Belt" and the oceangoing

President Xi Jinping and President Barack Obama in Sunnylands, California, 2013.

"21st Century Maritime Silk Road" are China's strategies for playing a bigger role in global affairs. China has expressed willingness to commit as much as $1.4 trillion to its "One Belt, One Road" strategy. To put this in perspective, it is more than ten times America's historic commitment to the Marshall Plan, which totaled $120 billion in today's dollars. China has an ambition to build 81,000 kilometers (about 50,000 miles) of high-speed railways connecting itself to most of Asia and Europe. One trunk route is to go from Kunming through Southeast Asia to Singapore. A second will cross the Karakorum Mountains and branch into two lines: one reaching Pakistani ports on the Arabian Sea; the other crossing Iran to Turkey, the Mediterranean, the Black Sea, and Southeastern Europe, with a branch connection to the Arabian Peninsula. A third trunk will go through Kazakhstan and Russia to Western Europe. China's plan is to enable train travel from London to Beijing in a mere two days as early as 2025.[4]

The PRC's GDP grew at an average of 10 percent a year from 1982 to 2011, even faster than the long growth spells of Japan (6.5 percent, 1951–1980) and South Korea (7.7 percent, 1966–1995). China's 2001 admission into the World Trade Organization has only served to accelerate that growth. The World Bank now estimates that exports represent a quarter of China's GDP, five times the level of 1978. By 2010, China's economy had become the second-largest in the world, only behind the United States, and if its moderate growth continues it will assume the top spot in just a few years. Based on purchasing power parity (PPP)—a calculation that equalizes the purchasing power of different currencies in their home countries for a given basket of goods—China may already have the world's largest economy, although in per capita terms it is still in the lower-middle-income bracket. The restructuring of the economy and resulting efficiency gains have contributed to a more than tenfold increase in GDP since 1978. China has succeeded in lifting 600 million people out of abject poverty since the reforms began.

The Shanghai Skyline at Night—the Oriental Pearl TV Tower (tallest left), Jinmao Tower (tallest second right) and the Shanghai World Financial Center (tallest right) in Lujiazui Financial District in Pudong, Shanghai, China. Shanghai currently remains China's economic and commercial center. Photo © Imaginechina.

The "miracle" comes with a heavy price. While living standards have improved for most people and a growing number of Chinese are getting rich, the income gap between rich and poor is widening, as is the gap between urban and rural areas. In China, the Gini coefficient has reached over 0.45, indicating a very uneven distribution of income. In addition, much of China's natural environment has been destroyed in the process of fast economic growth.

China's market reform was incremental, unlike Soviet-style of "shock therapy." China's transformation was pragmatic and based on local conditions since Deng Xiaoping was trying to build "socialism with Chinese characteristics." Different from the Soviet Union's political and economic reforms under Mikhail Gorbachev, Deng's economic reform adopted a step-by-step approach. The scope and pace of liberalization were carefully controlled and sometimes halted by conservatives in the party. Economic liberalization was first implemented and tested in a few provinces or SEZs. Only after these regions were successful were reform measures introduced and developed in the rest of the country.

The process of industrialization and structural change in China has been part of a general economic transition from a centrally planned to a market economy. Policy support has consisted of gradual and selective adoption of regulations in accordance with the appropriate pace and pattern of the transition. Key elements have been a reduction of the role of state-owned enterprises (SOEs); the gradual and selective introduction of market incentives through the regulatory reform of price systems; and government control of domestic labor mobility, external trade, and FDI. The share of SOEs in gross industrial output declined from 77 percent in 1978 to 50 percent in 1998 and 26 percent in 2011. It is projected to drop to around 10 percent by 2030. Meanwhile, the private sector has become a vibrant economic force, especially in IT sectors. Companies such as Alibaba, Xiaomi, Tencent and Huawei have become globally competitive.

Fixed investment that benefited from preferential credit, mainly from state-owned banks, grew very quickly between the late 1980s and the late 1990s and was directed at targeted industries and sectors. Moreover, manufacturing industries enjoyed tax incentives more favorable than those imposed on other industries. The economy has been heavily influenced by sizable public investment in physical infrastructure, direct government financing, the provision of credit at preferential interest rates, and tax rebates. In the absence of an efficient domestic securities market, bank loans have been the major source of corporate finance.

The government has influenced the sectoral distribution of FDI inflows. Guidelines and regulations were issued whereby FDI inflows were categorized as "prohibited," "permitted," or "encouraged." In the encouraged type, such as high-tech industries, incentives were given through extensive policies of preferential treatment such as tax rebates and/or exemptions, duty-free imports of capital equipment, and better access to public infrastructure and utilities. Administrative procedures were also streamlined for "free trade and high-technology development zones," and incentive packages were provided, including heavily subsidized land and energy provisions.

Prior to its accession to the WTO, China's trade policy was very industry selective, with extensive import restrictions, in order to support industrial restructuring. First, gradual and phased trade liberalization enabled imports of technology that China would not otherwise have had access to and were essential to making structural changes in Chinese industry. Second, foreign trade allowed the exportation of surplus production without which these structural changes, based on a combination of a large surplus of labor and rapidly increasing investment, would not have been sustainable. Exporting firms benefited from various pricing, tax, and loan privileges, as well as support for technological upgrades.

With the deepening of its economic reforms and, in particular, the decentralization of foreign trade, which has led to a massive entrance of private enterprises, many of the incentives have been phased out, nontariff barriers have been gradually dismantled, and tariff barriers have been significantly lowered.[5] Meanwhile, foreign investors began to complain about growing protectionism and rampant intellectual right piracy in China.

Privatization was gradual and even controversial in China. Private ownership was legalized when the Property Law of the People's Republic of China was adopted by the National People's Congress, China's legislative body, and went into effect on October 1, 2007.

The law is a milestone on the path toward a market economy. The legislation stopped short of abrogating the principle that all land belongs to the state, a fundamental part of the communist system since 1949. But it broke ground by establishing new protections for private homes and businesses and for farmers with long-term leases on their fields. These goals had long been sought by the entrepreneurs who now account for more than half of China's production, by the swiftly climbing number of urban families that have bought their own apartments, and by the millions of farmers whose croplands have come under growing pressure from real estate developers.

One of the keys to success in China's economic reform has been the willingness to experiment, to try different approaches to solving common problems and then evaluate the results free of political dogma. Deng Xiaoping's pragmatic policies were essential in China's transition from a tightly controlled planned economy to the large market sector of today.

THE BEIJING CONSENSUS?

Neither coined nor endorsed by the Chinese government, the term *Beijing Consensus* gained popularity in international political economy. It was first suggested in 2004 by Joshua Cooper Ramo, a journalist-editor, to summarize the developmental model based on economic liberalization under tight political control.

Does the Chinese model represent something vastly different from the Japanese or Korean model? Does it challenge the *Washington Consensus*, which suggests that the best way to achieve economic growth is through the adoption of a series of liberal, free-market, economic and political policies?

49

Whether the *Beijing Consensus* challenges the *Washington Consensus* or not remains a policy debate, but already some developing countries in Africa and Latin America seem very interested in this Chinese development path.

Deng Xiaoping is often compared to Mikhail Gorbachev as both were creative leaders who tried to reform a communist system. Gorbachev introduced *glasnost* (political openness) and *perestroika* (economic restructuring) simultaneously, reform policies that unleashed forces leading to the demise of the Soviet Union. In contrast, Deng believed it was important to maintain the party's dominance, which was crucial for creating a stable social environment for economic development. By choosing to start with economic reform and introducing it very cautiously, the Chinese Communist Party had a greater capacity to manage the change, and China's economy prospered without fundamentally changing the country's political structure. But is such a strategy sustainable?

Much of the Washington consensus was right, especially the points that focused on sound macroeconomic policies such as fiscal discipline and public expenditures on health care, education, and infrastructure. Indeed, China itself has followed some of these macroeconomic policies. Clearly, one should not look at China's experience from the dichotomy of the *Beijing Consensus* versus the *Washington Consensus*. China's development, with its different political and economic approaches, is more complicated than a single model can describe.

MAJOR DEVELOPMENT CHALLENGES AHEAD

The speed of China's progression from a low-income, populous country to a global economic force has continued to astound many analysts and observers. Academics and policymakers in the developed and developing world continue to examine China's progress and its impact on regional and world economies.

A growing China has growing pains. Its prosperous surface masks a rising sea of problems and challenges. China's economic achievements since the late 1970s have made its development experience distinct in many ways from those of many other economies. Its robust economic growth, which has brought the country to the status of one of the largest economies in the world, has dramatically reduced poverty. However, analysts in China are still grappling with various questions: How can growth be more sustainable? What can be done to close the remaining gap between China and the world's leading economies? How can welfare benefits for its population be further enhanced? How can environmental challenges be addressed? How will

China move from reliance on labor-intensive, cheap goods to developing its brand names based on high technology, as did Japan, South Korea, and Taiwan?

Behind the dazzling skylines and impressive statistics, another reality exists in China, one replete with unresolved problems and daunting numbers that suggest a far darker scenario. For example, China must create some 12 to 15 million new jobs annually just to keep up with population growth; the government must deal with a growing number of unemployed or underemployed people as a result of slower growth; and a "floating population" (rural workers who have moved to the cities to find work) of about 270 million, the largest migration in human history, has posed challenges in multiple areas such as social stability, welfare, education, and urbanization. These migrants have no job security, no long-term housing, and no health care; China has no functioning pension system, and the cost of creating one is estimated to be in the hundreds of billions of dollars.[6] In addition, rising labor cost and a declining and graying population will affect long-term growth. On the other hand, a new middle class eager to protect its newfound property and quality of life is beginning to challenge government policies.

While China has overcome many difficulties in the process of rapid economic growth, the country is still faced with many problems. Some are the unavoidable consequences of the ongoing transition from central planning, while others have emerged in the process of development. Some are strictly domestic, while others involve external relations. Some have not been encountered by other East Asian economies, including greater pressure to comply with international trade rules, to improve human rights, and to democratize. Several major challenges particularly need to be addressed.

One of the biggest challenges for China is to bring the political system more into line with the economic system. Can a "harmonious society," as advocated by former President Hu Jintao, be established without political reform? Modernization theories suggest that as a society develops, a rising middle class will serve as the stimulus for a democratic movement. Singapore is an obvious exception, and China could prove these modernization theories wrong again. China's somewhat unique combination of state-led, market-based, economic development and a socialist legacy give most socioeconomic sectors, especially the growing middle class, an interest in maintaining the political status quo since this is the group that benefits the most from the current political and economic structure.

The movement that culminated in the 1989 Tiananmen Square incident, understood in the West as a pro-democracy movement, started in Beijing and other large cities as college students went to the streets to express their frustration over such social problems as rising prices, poor treatment of intellectuals, and rampant corruption. With the booming economy and the loosening of government controls, corruption has grown in a seemingly greater proportion than the economy. Widespread corruption not only threatens to erode the foundation of the Chinese economy but also tarnishes China's and the Communist Party's image.

While the overall economic reforms have been undertaken effectively, financial reform has received a low priority. With bad debts and real estate bubbles, China's fragile financial system may not withstand major economic fluctuations if the global economy slows down in the future. In 2008, as the global economic downturn hit China, Chinese exports declined for the first time in seven years. China's growth rate dropped to around 7 percent in 2015 and is expected to drop further—the so-called "new normal" of slower growth.

Uneven Development

As liberalization and marketization continued, the economic winners and losers began to emerge. Economic opportunities were skewed in favor of those with *guanxi*, or political and social connections.

China is rapidly urbanizing. It is moving from a peasant society to an industrial powerhouse. The *hukou* system no longer restricts movement from rural to urban areas. As late as the 1980s, 80 percent of the population lived in rural areas. By the 2010s, it had dropped to under 50 percent. China is experiencing a growing development gap between coastal and inland and urban and rural areas. Because market-based operations have expanded, inequality in the distribution of income and wealth is likely to increase in the near future. Despite the overall enhancement of standards of living, China is missing social safety nets that could support the most disadvantaged groups in the society.

Class issues have grown as a result of uneven economic development. An underclass of migrant workers—the "floating population"—has developed, not only creating infrastructure challenges to the cities but more seriously perpetuating the division between rich and poor and creating social tensions. These internal migrants who have relocated from rural to urban areas not only are looked down on by urban residents but do not enjoy the same level of social benefits. Their children cannot enroll in urban public schools. As has happened during industrialization worldwide, migration to the cities has also served to break up the traditional family and community structures that

Palace Museum, Beijing, in heavy smog. According to the World Health Organization (WHO), seventeen of the twenty most polluted cities in the world are located in China. Photo © Imaginechina.

have been the basis of much of Chinese culture. China also needs to sustain adequate job growth for tens of millions of workers laid off from SOEs, migrants, and new entrants to the workforce such as college graduates.

Mass protests have become common in contemporary China. According to official statistics, in 2004 there were 74,000 "mass incidents" (demonstrations and riots), an increase from 58,000 the year before and only 10,000 a decade ago. By the early 2010s, such protests had climbed to over 150,000 annually. In addition, a sharp rise in crime rates is eroding the stability of Chinese society.

Environmental Degradation

After three decades of rapid economic development, most of China's rivers are black with industrial and human waste. Just two decades ago many of these rivers were clean enough for drinking and swimming. In many Chinese cities, it is hard to see a blue sky even on a sunny day. According to the World Health Organization (WHO), seventeen of the twenty most polluted cities in the world are located in China. China also boasts one-third of the world's cigarette smokers. By early 2008, it had replaced the United States as the world's largest emitter of carbon dioxide, the main greenhouse gas. Despite strenuous efforts, Beijing's air quality was only moderately improved during

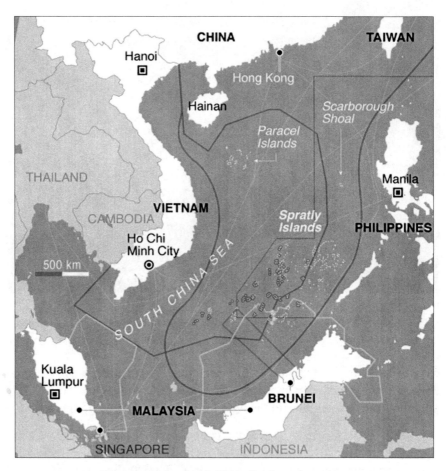

Disputes in the South China Sea have become a
source of instability in East Asia.

the 2008 Summer Olympics, and heavy air pollution returned to Beijing
shortly after the games.

During the November 2014 APEC summit in Beijing, blue sky
temporarily reappeared in Beijing due to the government's emission
reduction campaign. President Xi Jinping asserted that China should do more
and try to let the "APEC blue" stay. However, the smog was so heavy that
in December 2015 the Beijing city government issued its first red alert for
pollution, ordering schools to close, halting outdoor construction, restricting
car use, and banning fireworks and outdoor barbecues due to hazardous air
quality. Deterioration of the environment—most notably air pollution, soil
erosion, and a steady fall in the water table, especially in the north—is a

long-term problem. China continues to lose arable land because of erosion and economic development.

International Image

China's rapid economic growth has been met with mixed feelings. Some countries view China's development as an opportunity; others feel threatened by the competition. By 2011, China had accumulated a foreign exchange reserve of over $3 trillion. While the United States and other Western economies have been pressuring the Chinese government to appreciate its currency as they did to Japan in the 1980s, many economists worry that a sharp rise in the yuan may trigger an economic crisis in China similar to what happened in Japan after the 1985 Plaza Accord. External pressure for currency revaluation mounted in light of China's expanding trade surplus, as was the case in Japan in the mid-1980s. The Chinese government let the yuan appreciate around 30 percent after 2005. In May 2015, the IMF declared that the yuan was no longer undervalued, and in November 2015, the IMF included the yuan in the Special Drawing Rights (SDR) basket of reserve currencies, along with the US dollar, British pound, Japanese yen, and euro, paving the way for broader use of the *renminbi* in trade and finance and securing China's standing as a global economic power. However, some analysts believe that the Chinese government continues to control the financial market.

In addition to economic issues, China is also facing serious challenges in its foreign policy. As tensions grew in the South China Sea and East China Sea in the first half of the 2010s, China suffered a huge blow in its international image since its actions in the disputed areas were considered to be aggressive by many. In September 2015 Beijing staged a massive military parade to mark the 70th anniversary of the end of WWII and Anti-Japanese War when Japan-China relations were in desperate need of improvement. Though the Chinese government said it was not aimed at Japan, the parade was not well received outside China. China has also been suspected of hacking into its rivals' computer systems to steal commercial and national security secrets.

5

COMPARING EAST ASIAN ECONOMIES

E ast Asian nations that have managed to succeed since the end of World
War II have arguably followed a roughly similar process, with rapid
growth occurring under a strong or authoritarian regime, democratization
occurring later at higher levels of development, and reforms implemented
that are aimed at strengthening existing economic and political institutions.
To understand East Asian development models, one has to study the
role of the state in shaping the market and vice versa. The East Asian
economies did not grow in a vacuum; one also needs to understand how
the international political and economic environments shaped East Asia's
development. How these economies were affected by and coped with the
1997–98 Asian financial crisis and the 2008-2010 global recession also
needs to be studied. However, the East Asian economies did not all chart
the same linear pattern. Some features of the economic development of
these nations are converging whereas others are diverging.

The state and the market are two central concepts in international
political economy. East Asian economies are similar in that they are
production-oriented, export-led, and state-directed. They have also
invested heavily in human resources and R&D. They share some of the
following major features.

SIMILARITIES

Export-Oriented Policies and "Going Global" Strategies

All the East Asian nations have manufacturing-based trading economies.
The export-oriented strategy seemed to be the only realistic route for
resource-poor South Korea, Taiwan, and Japan, but the PRC, with richer
resources, has also adopted this strategy. It is interesting to compare South
Korea, Taiwan, and Japan, which turned their resource paucity into an
advantage for development, with developing countries in regions such
as Africa, which have suffered from the so-called resource curse despite

their abundance of natural resources. Resource curse refers to the paradox that countries with an abundance of natural resources tend to have less economic growth than countries without these natural resources. Unlike the case in Africa, the East Asian economies have taken advantage of their strength in human capital and become successful trading powers.

The East Asian economies began to invest and purchase overseas after they had accumulated foreign currency reserves as a result of robust exports. From Japan's purchase of the Rockefeller Center in New York and several Hollywood movie studios to China's purchase of shares in Morgan Stanley and Blackstone and its global investments, Asian economies are going global and acquiring foreign assets.

Stable Domestic Conditions

Economic development cannot be achieved without stable political and social environments. All East Asian countries have relatively peaceful and orderly societies. Japan and South Korea enjoyed a long period of domestic stability after World War II and the Korean War respectively. Taiwan's society stabilized by 1950 after initial conflicts with the arrival of the KMT government. The island's people had the common goal of seeking survival and development, and a competitive spirit was instilled in the whole society. With the situation across the Taiwan Strait so confrontational during those years, all residents were especially willing to work together wholeheartedly for common economic development. It is therefore little wonder that Taiwan was able to recover so quickly from the ravages of war. The PRC's domestic situation finally stabilized after Mao Zedong's death in 1976 and the end of the Cultural Revolution. Like the others, the PRC began to focus on economic reconstruction after political stability was achieved.

The Active Role of the State

Originated in Japan, developmental state capitalism was widely embraced by the East Asian economies, whose governments actively interacted with markets. The government provided directions for the economy by participating directly or indirectly in basic economic activities, such as building infrastructure and establishing a legal system, and by coordinating or guiding private sector activities.

When the PRC introduced economic reforms in the late 1970s, its political system was intact. The central government or the state machinery was in full control of provincial and local governments in China. Centrally planned practices and institutions were maintained before new market institutions were created. The state fully supported reform initiatives and provided assistance to ensure that they could be carried out smoothly. State policies included maintaining law and order, enforcing rules and regulations, establishing and improving institutional frameworks to suit the new environment, and providing public infrastructure such as roads, schools, and hospitals to the masses. China's strong state and institutional capacity played a crucial role in creating a climate conducive to growth at the initial stage of reform.

State involvement in economic development includes the articulation of national economic goals, the establishment of specialized bureaucracies, the creation of targeted industrial sectors and export-processing zones, and the willingness to thwart popular political resistance. The 1997 financial crisis facilitated the transformation of a developmental state into a welfare state in South Korea and Japan by bringing social inequality to the forefront of political debate and paving the way for new and more effective welfare policies. The state has also played a very important role in Taiwan's economic development. Before the 1980s, because of the security threat from the PRC, the Taiwanese government had the power to maintain a stable society with strict law and order. This was a necessary condition for both attracting investment and sustaining a good living environment. As tensions with the PRC abated in the 1980s and afterward, the government's authoritarian style was gradually replaced with democratic politics.

To cope with the global economic recession—triggered by the U.S. subprime mortgage crisis that became apparent in 2007—these Asian governments passed economic stimulus packages in 2008 and 2009. Yet people expect more from their governments, partly because they have become accustomed to active state intervention in the economies. At the beginning of 2009, for example, both Prime Minister Aso Taro of Japan and President Lee Myung-bak of South Korea had very low approval ratings for their ineffective measures to deal with the crisis and were under pressure to resign. Aso stepped down in September 2009 when his LDP lost to DPJ in the parliamentary election. Likewise, lackluster performance by the KMT government to boost living standards of ordinary people in Taiwan led to its losing power to the DPP in 2016.

Visionary Individual Leaders

Individuals can shape the course of history. In East Asia, the role of far-sighted and determined leaders such as Yoshida Shigeru, Park Chung-hee, Deng Xiaoping, and Chiang Kai-shek cannot be underestimated in helping their economies take off.

Yoshida's well-designed domestic and foreign policies became the guiding principle of Japan's postwar economic recovery. Park Chung-hee's industrialization policy and export-promoting strategy helped turn South Korean *chaebols* into globally competitive enterprises later. Chiang Kai-shek strengthened Taiwan's economic base while consolidating its defense, and his son Chiang Ching-kuo gradually opened up Taiwanese society by allowing the existence of opposition parties, eventually turning Taiwan into a free and prosperous society. "To get rich is glorious," claimed Deng Xiaoping, who encouraged the Chinese to work hard and prosper and introduced privatization policies. In rural areas, the "household responsibility system" was adopted and replaced the communes. What food peasants grew beyond the government quota was sold on free markets. This system was later extended to other sectors of the economy, and local managers were held responsible for the profits and losses of their enterprises.

Investment in Human Resources

Inspiration and perspiration are both needed if a society is to progress. Although cultural determinist views are controversial for their exaggeration of cultural differences and their selective focus on some aspects of a culture, the success of the East Asian countries has been attributed in part to the impact of Confucianism and "Asian values," which include an emphasis on education, hard work, a relatively high level of individual savings, a nationalistic desire for a strong state, and a willingness to sacrifice personal interest for the good of society.

Increased productivity is often the result of improvements in education and skills. In both quantity and quality, the East Asian economies have made a major commitment to education and training. For example, in what has been described by the United Nations Educational, Scientific, and Cultural Organization (UNESCO) as "clearly the great experiment in the mass education in the history of the world," literacy rates in China increased from 20 percent in 1949 to 65 percent by the end of the 1970s. China's literacy rate continued to soar as the country reopened its economy to the world. In comparison, India's literacy rate stood at 41 percent at the end of the 1970s.[1] A solid educational foundation helps immensely in the absorption of new ideas and the coordination of government policies. As science and technology improved, Taiwan extended compulsory

Pedestrians walk past a big propaganda billboard with the portrait of Deng Xiaoping in Shenzhen city, Guangdong province, January, 2009. The roles played by leaders such as Deng Xiaoping, Yoshida Shigeru, and Chiang Kai-shek in regard to transforming their countries' economies cannot be underestimated. Photo © Imaginechina.

education to nine years in 1968. Meanwhile, additional technological and vocational colleges were established to meet the needs of an industrial sector that was being continuously upgraded. The biggest investment of most families in East Asia is their children's education. Today all these East Asian economies boast some of the best skilled labor forces in the world.

These East Asian economies also face demographic challenges such as graying and declining populations. Population and immigration policies have been heatedly debated in these countries. In China's case, the government scraped the "one child" policy in 2015 and allowed each couple to have two children.

MAJOR DIFFERENCES

Despite the above-mentioned similarities, the development paths of East Asia's economies demonstrate clear differences. These differences are more salient between the PRC and the other three economies.

The External Environment

South Korea and Taiwan are important cases for understanding the role of outside powers. During their authoritarian periods, both South Korea and Taiwan were under American protection. Without the support provided by the U.S. military and American markets, they probably could not have remained independent as late as the early 1980s. The American policy of engagement with these regimes gave the United States the ability to nudge things forward at crucial junctures. The United States was also important as a locus for exiles and a transmitter of ideas and values, and many Taiwanese and Korean leaders studied in the West. Likewise, the U.S. security umbrella obviously provided an important benefit to Japan, relieving it of the need to fund its own security during the early years of postwar reconstruction. Benign international conditions were extremely conducive to the success of these economies, especially the postwar free trade regime. However, outsiders can only play a role by providing resources, ideas, and strategies. Ultimately it is up to local actors to make democracy work.[2]

While Taiwan and South Korea largely followed Japan's developmental state model, the PRC's growth since the 1970s faced different international political and economic conditions. As the latest developer among the four, the PRC has pursued a more market-focused economic policy characterized by relative independence of private businesses rather than statist development strategies. Without security guarantees such as those enjoyed by Japan, South Korea, and Taiwan, the PRC had to build a peaceful regional and international environment for its own economic development, which is why throughout the 1980s and 1990s the PRC developed friendly ties with great powers and its Asian neighbors, following Deng Xiaoping's dictum of keeping a low profile in international affairs. Japanese policies were often strongly "anti-market," insulating numerous domestic sectors from international competition and protecting an increasing number of globally noncompetitive firms, such as construction and food processing, at high costs to domestic consumers.[3] Thus, China had to focus on both the international and domestic dimensions whereas the other East Asian economies could largely afford to focus on domestic conditions alone.

Income Distribution

A major feature of the East Asian model is the achievement of high growth with equity. Growth in Japan, South Korea, and Taiwan was attained in tandem with relatively high levels of social and economic equality.

High levels economic growth also created a large middle class in these economies, where a civil society emerged and expanded.

By contrast, China's growth has been achieved at the expense of a widening income gap and a worsening of the natural environment. China's trajectory is a departure from other East Asian nations' mixture of high growth with social equality. With its wide discrepancy between rich and poor, China is more like a developing country in regions such as Latin America. The Chinese middle class generally enjoys the status quo, so it is unrealistic to rely on the nouveau riche to push for democratization in China.

When Deng Xiaoping said "To get rich is glorious," he was encouraging a small minority of the population to become rich, hoping that they would help raise the living standards of the rest of the population. The strategy was only partially successful. A small group has indeed prospered, but many Chinese, especially those living in the vast countryside and inland provinces, remain poor. How to achieve more even development is a major challenge facing China in the twenty-first century.

The PRC Factor

China's economic development exhibits several distinct features. First, China's economy did not really take off until after 1978 when Japan, Taiwan and South Korea were already enjoying high standards of living. In just over two decades, China's economy became one of the largest in the world. Second, it has employed a mixture of strategies, including central planning, inward-oriented import-substitution industrialization along with a strong export orientation, and encouragement of foreign direct investment (FDI). Throughout the 1990s and 2000s, the PRC has been the largest recipient of FDI among developing economies. Taiwan and South Korea have also been receptive to FDI. By contrast, Japan has largely resisted it. Third, the PRC has continuously modified its policies, in a creative and innovative manner, in accordance with the prevailing development strategy and the changing domestic and international environments. This was particularly the case in the run-up to and aftermath of its accession to the WTO in 2001.

Although it trades extensively with other Asian economies, the PRC has also become a serious competitor with them. The PRC has been remarkably successful in attracting FDI, and foreign-owned firms have been a key driver of the growth of high-value-added Chinese exports. Unlike the Indian diaspora, the Chinese diaspora played a crucial role in providing capital for investment after China initiated its economic reforms in the late 1970s. China established four SEZs in the early 1980s on the country's southeast coast, taking advantage of their proximity to Taiwan, Hong Kong, Macao, and Southeast Asia, where large numbers of overseas Chinese were eager to invest in their ancestral homeland. According to Xinhua, China's official news agency, in 2007 China attracted $74.77 billion in FDI and ranked first in FDI among developing nations for the fifteenth year in a row. In 2010, FDI in China reached a record high of $105.7 billion. Meanwhile, China began to invest abroad in the 1990s, and from 2000 to 2014, Chinese firms spent nearly $46 billion on new establishments and acquisitions in the U.S. By 2020 the U.S. could receive between $100-200 billion of Chinese investment, according to a study by the National Committee on U.S.-China Relations and the Rhodium Group.

China's economic growth rate had been around 10 percent for thirty years before it slowed down in the 2010s. The Chinese authorities have been struggling to cool down the growth and investment rates in order to deflect inflationary pressures. Since opening its markets to international trade and joining the WTO, China has emerged as a manufacturing powerhouse, playing a central role in the global supply chain for a wide range of products. This process is providing substantial benefits to China and the Asian region in general as China imports components such as computer chips and auto parts from its neighbors for use in its export industries. China's emergence as a major manufacturing center also poses competitive challenges for its neighbors, which need to adjust to this new feature of the environment.

China has been a growth engine for many other nations. For example, in 1992 China-ROK trade was only $6 billion. That number skyrocketed to over $274 billion in 2013 and topped $300 billion in 2014, larger than South Korea's trade with the U.S. and Japan combined. China has been South Korea's largest trading partner since 2004. Chinese tourists have been the largest group of foreign visitors to South Korea for years. During President Xi Jinping's July 2014 visit to Seoul, the two countries agreed to set up direct won-yuan trading, which made the Chinese yuan the only currency directly convertible with the won except the U.S. dollar. The two countries also signed a free trade agreement in 2015. Chinese tourists' impressive purchasing power has been welcomed by countries in Asia and beyond.

China's role as a regional manufacturing hub has led to significant intraregional investment flows. Large firms in the region, many of them headquartered in South Korea, Taiwan, and Japan, have moved parts of their production processes to the Chinese mainland. However, as Chinese labor is becoming more expensive, both Chinese and foreign firms are increasingly turning to Vietnam, Bangladesh, Sri Lanka, and other even lower labor economies.

Other Factors

South Korea's and Japan's economies are led by industrial conglomerates. Taiwan also has large industrial conglomerates such as world-leading microchip producer, Taiwan Semiconductor Manufacturing Corporation. However, family-owned small and medium sized enterprises are particularly important in Taiwan and played a vital role in Taiwan's economic take-off. All East Asian economies are export-oriented, boasting strong information technology (IT) sectors and depending heavily on the U.S. and Chinese markets. Japan, South Korea, and Taiwan had to overcome the obstacle of limited natural resources in rebuilding their war-torn economies. South Korea and Taiwan were in the vanguard when the "third wave" of democratization reached the region in the late 1980s.[4] By the early twenty-first century, both democracies had been consolidated.

The East Asian economies also fared differently during the Asian financial crisis of 1997. What happened in East Asia is not peculiar and had already occurred in many Latin American countries in the 1980s. These economies faced sudden currency depreciations due to speculative attacks or large outflows of funds. The crisis began in Thailand and spread to other Southeast Asian nations before it hit Northeast Asia. South Korea suffered tremendously, and thousands of small and medium-sized companies were plunged into bankruptcy. The IMF's short-term macroeconomic policy for Korea was to call for a budget deficit reduction (by raising taxes and cutting government spending) and a tighter monetary policy (with higher interest rates and less credit availability), which together depressed growth and raised unemployment.

The Japanese yen dropped sharply during the financial crisis, causing grave concerns that this would trigger a deeper Asian crisis or world recession. Yet neither the IMF nor Western leaders had asked Japan to increase its interest rate (which at 0.5 percent was among the lowest in the world) to defend the yen. Instead they wanted Japan to take fiscal measures to expand the economy. This tolerance of low interest rates in Japan, as well as pressure on the government to pump up its economy, was

The 2008 Summer Olympics in Beijing—a night view of the National Stadium, known as the "Birds Nest," in Beijing, China, August 2008. Photo © Imaginechina.

a very different approach than the high-interest, austerity-budget medicine prescribed for the other ailing East Asian countries.

Helped by their huge foreign exchange reserves, China, Taiwan, and Japan weathered the crisis better than South Korea. In China, whose currency was not freely traded due to tight control by the government, the yuan did not depreciate. As a result, China was barely hit by the financial crisis. It was the rapid buildup of external debt that more than anything else led to the crisis in Thailand, Indonesia, Malaysia, and South Korea. One of the lessons learned is that developing countries should not build up a large foreign debt even if they have relatively large export earnings.

A final interesting comparative point is the question of whether hosting the Olympics can help countries democratize and become fully integrated into the international political and economic system. To a great extent, the 1964 Tokyo Summer Olympics symbolized Japan's formal reentry into the international system where it would play a constructive role. It provided an opportunity to display Japan's industrial and technological achievements to the world, including the high-speed "bullet train" (*shinkansen* 新干线) system. The 1988 Seoul Summer Olympics served as a catalyst for South Korea's economic development. It also provided an opportunity for South Korea to shake off authoritarian rule and move toward democracy. China staged a spectacular global sporting event in the summer of 2008, but the Beijing Olympics apparently has had limited impact on China's democratization so far.

6

TOWARD A COMPREHENSIVE UNDERSTANDING OF EAST ASIA'S ECONOMIC "MIRACLES"

E ast Asian nations made impressive progress in promoting economic growth after World War II. Although each has its unique features, lumped together, they are considered the "East Asian miracle" in international political economy. Although the 1997–98 Asian financial crisis led some people to think that the miracle was no more than a mirage, East Asia remains one of the most dynamic and prosperous regions in the world. No one can underestimate the importance of East Asian economies to global development. While thriftiness is deeply rooted in many Asian cultures and people do save a lot in East Asian countries, their purchasing power cannot be underestimated. One only needs to look at the omnipresent well-to-do tourists from Japan, Taiwan, South Korea, and the Chinese mainland. Top tourist destinations such as Hawaii and Paris are particularly eager to attract the nouveau riche from China now.

What explains East Asia's economic success? Is the East Asian model sustainable? Economist and syndicated columnist Paul Krugman argued in 1994 that East Asia's rapid growth in output was nothing extraordinary and could be fully explained by the rapid growth of inputs: expansion of employment, increases in education levels, massive investments in physical capital, and the willingness to save (i.e., to sacrifice current consumption for the sake of future production). These strategies, he suggested, were no different from the Soviet growth model of the 1950s and 1960s.[1] According to Krugman, Asian growth was "mainly a matter of perspiration rather than inspiration—of working harder, not smarter."[2]

That the Soviet Union has collapsed and East Asian economies continue to be very vibrant indicates that the comparison is problematic. Krugman's interpretation of the Soviet model was that it was driven by perspiration not inspiration. He mistakenly suggested that Singapore's growth could be explained entirely by increases in measured inputs such as the amount of production and that there was no sign of increased efficiency. This interpretation has been proven wrong by developments in Japan, South Korea, Taiwan, Hong Kong, and Singapore, as these economies have become high-tech with extraordinary productivity and efficiency. Even China, the latest developer among these economies, is focusing on innovation and attempting to build its own brand of automobiles and jumbo passenger airplanes. China has already built the world's most extensive high-speed railway system and has begun to help other countries to develop such modern infrastructure.

THE STATE AND THE MARKET

Are there secrets to East Asia's continued growth? An emphasis on education, the inclination to save, and an export priority policy seem to be some common strategies adopted by these economies. But there are more. From an international political economy perspective, what are the roles of government and the market in explaining the East Asian success and how has globalization affected development in East Asia?

China's stock market jitters in summer 2015 and the Chinese government's intervention to stabilize the market illustrated tensions between market and state and renewed debate about the roles of the two. Scholars and policymakers have reached no consensus on the roles of the government and the market in East Asian economic development. Two competing views have shaped inquiries into the source of the rapid growth of East Asian economies and efforts to derive lessons for other developing economies: the market-friendly view, according to which government intervenes little in the market; and the developmental state view, in which the state governs and guides the market. Proponents of the former view see the East Asian story as a vindication of liberal free-market principles, while defenders of the latter view attribute the success of these countries to active and effective government intervention. Interestingly, they share the conception that the market and government are alternative mechanisms for resource allocation in economic development. They are different only in their judgment of the extent to which market failures have been, and ought to be, remedied by direct government intervention. Clearly, both state and market are powerful forces in East Asia's growth. They coexist and interact and form the main institutions that shape economic development.

A third view has been developed by scholars who turn their attention to the way economic decisions were shared and divided between the market and public administration. They recognize that East Asia has strong social capital—social networks among people that can increase productivity both individually and collectively—and institutional foundations for proper development and that the strong role of government or the market might not be the major cause. They have suggested the so-called market-enhancing theory or the synergy between market and government.[3] Instead of viewing government and the market as mutually exclusive substitutes, they examine the capacity of government policy to facilitate or complement private sector coordination. They start from the premise that private sector institutions have important comparative advantages over government, particularly in their ability to quickly process information. At the same time, these analysts recognize that the capabilities of the private sector are limited in developing economies.

There are other explanations for East Asia's spectacular growth. Some scholars have emphasized the role of war in East Asia's development.[4] Wars create states and economies and are powerful agents for political, economic, and social change. These scholars contend that World War II, the Korean War, the Vietnam War, and the constant competition (and preparation for war) between the two Koreas and two Chinas have all stimulated economic growth and social transformations in East Asia. For example, Japan's economy benefited enormously from military procurements during the Korean and Vietnam wars. The Korean War was described by Prime Minister Yoshida Shigeru as "a gift of the gods" in Japan's post–World War II recovery and growth, and large American procurements during the Vietnam War provided additional demand for Japanese goods, which helped sustain the high growth of the 1960s. The almost five-decade Cold War ensured long-term American assistance to and protection of Japan.

The discussion of the economies of East Asia reveals a rich diversity of national systems of political economy in the region. Japan demilitarized and democratized shortly after its surrender at the end of World War II. With the help of the United States, it was quickly integrated into Western political and economic systems. South Korea and Taiwan were authoritarian and military dictatorships when their economies began to take off. They democratized only after their economies had reached a higher level. The PRC's economic reforms have been overseen by the Communist Party of China. Despite some procedural reforms within the party, including membership for entrepreneurs, China's one-party political structure remains unchanged nearly forty years after the economic reforms were launched (see Table 6.1)

Table 6.1. Do Political Democracy and
Economic Growth Go Hand in Hand?

	Democracy?	Economic Take-off	Recognized as Democracy
Japan	yes	early 1950s	early 1950s
South Korea	yes	late 1960s	late 1980s
Taiwan	yes	late 1960s	early 1990s
PRC	no	early 1980s	???

In addition to market, state, and war, many other factors have been identified as reasons for East Asia's success—outward policy orientations, high saving and investment rates, an emphasis on achieving and learning, macroeconomic discipline, strong leadership, and external influences—although the relative weight of each in explaining the region's success is still a matter of considerable debate.

LEVELS OF ANALYSIS

To better understand the development trajectories of these East Asian economies, one may also use different levels of analysis to study their performances comparatively. Three levels can be analyzed: international, national (domestic), and individual.

International Conditions

East Asian nations' economic growth is inseparable from the external environment. Generally speaking, the international environment has been conducive to these economies as they attempted to maintain high growth rates. As in other regions, protectionist policies exist in East Asia to shelter domestic industries such as the agricultural sector from international competition. None of these Asian economies chose an isolationist path. Instead, they are very outward looking and welcome international trade and other international exchanges. East Asian economies embraced globalization and have benefited from integration into the global political economy.

The outside world has also generally supported and helped these economies to modernize. Japan, South Korea, and Taiwan received valuable political, military, and economic aid from the United States during the early stages of their economic development. The PRC was isolated by the West during much of the Cold War, but later it was assisted in reentering the international community in such matters as membership at the United Nations and WTO. All have had robust trading relations with the West. Japan, South Korea, and Taiwan have also helped the PRC to catch up. All three have invested heavily in the Chinese mainland, and Japan provided billions of dollars in government loans to China.

An interesting observation is that the Olympics have served as a coming-out party for these nations. From the 1964 summer games in Tokyo to the 1988 summer games in Seoul and the 2008 summer games in Beijing, the Olympics have come to these countries roughly every twenty years, which reflects the fact that their dates of economic takeoff are about twenty years apart. Preparation for the 2020 Tokyo Olympics may serve as a stimulus for the much-needed economic revival of Japan after over two decades of stagnation.

Domestic Policies

Political stability provided a necessary condition for economic growth. Although politicians in these countries have disagreed on what the best economic policy should be and how fast their economies should grow, they have all been committed to promoting economic development and improving living standards.

Beginning in the 1950s, East Asian countries adopted wide-ranging policies aimed at transforming themselves into market economies. Sound macroeconomic policies provided a stable backdrop for business growth. At an early stage, the importance of infrastructure investment as an aid to exporters and import-competing firms was recognized and appropriate measures taken. Later in the reform process greater emphasis was placed on liberalization of trade and financial sectors. The main thrust of economic policy became an outward orientation with strong incentives for exporters and a commitment to growth through trade.

Individual Leaders

Sound economic policies are made at the central level of government, often under the leadership of visionary individuals. National leaders must design policies that are most suitable for the nation. More important, these policies have to be effectively implemented, with an iron hand if necessary.

East Asia is fortunate to have had such individual leaders during the critical years of their economic growth. One can only imagine, without Deng Xiaoping's resolute policy of opening China to the West after Mao's death, how long the country would have struggled in its pursuit of modernization. Likewise, Yoshida Shigeru, Ikeda Hayato, Chiang Kai-shek, Chiang Ching-kuo, Syngman Rhee, and Park Chung-hee all played crucial roles during their countries' economic transformations.

Lessons for Other Developing Countries

Is there a singular East Asian development model? This booklet suggests that, although the four economies have some commonalities, their development paths are markedly different. While some attributes are possessed by all, such as an emphasis on education, a relatively high level of savings, and a strong work ethic, these economies have faced different domestic and international challenges; therefore, their policies have been different.

Japan was already an industrial power before World War II. With a solid industrial base, an economy-focused policy, and strong U.S. economic and military support, Japan's postwar recovery, though spectacular, was perhaps not surprising. South Korea and Taiwan followed a similar pattern of development. Protected and prodded by the United States, both designed export-oriented policies and closely linked their growth to the insatiable U.S. market. They confirm the democratization theory that suggests that a country can only move toward democracy when its economic development has reached a certain level. Both formally moved toward democratization in the 1980s after they had achieved impressive economic growth, although they had held elections before. In the twenty-first century, South Korea has skillfully managed relations with the United States and China, signing free trade agreements with both and participating in economic initiatives of both. Taiwan, due to security concerns and ideological conflict, has been struggling in dealing with China's rise.

The situation in the PRC is much more complicated. While sharing some of the development traits of the other three economies, the PRC is much bigger and does not fit any simple model. In fact, there are several Chinas: the coastal China that is quickly catching up with the "Asian tigers" and becoming increasingly cosmopolitan, the rust-belt China of the northeast that reflects the reality and dilemma of many state-owned enterprises in the competitive new economy, and the inland agricultural China that remains poor and underdeveloped.

The East Asian economies did not adopt greater outward orientation according to a common model or blueprint. Only Hong Kong and Singapore have adopted totally free trade policies with virtually no tariff or nontariff barriers. To varying degrees, the other newly industrializing economies (NIEs) in the region all adopted interventionist but market friendly policies, including export promotion and the creation of selective import barriers. These interventionist aspects of trade policy have had great appeal for a number of more recently emerging economies.

East Asia's experience suggests that political freedom is not a prerequisite for economic growth. The ability of a government to formulate sound economic policies is more important than the type of government. High economic performance will come from both democracies and authoritarian regimes that invest in human capital and physical infrastructure, encourage competition, maintain strong state institutions and legal systems, and adopt consistently sound policies. High savings and investment rates, accumulation of physical and human capital, and market-friendly government policies have all contributed to East Asia's success. China's impressive economic performance has renewed the interesting debate over democracy versus governance.

Many analysts, including Joseph Stiglitz—the Columbia University economics professor and former Senior Vice President and Chief Economist of the World Bank, argue that government intervention has played a critical role in East Asia's economic success. Governments in East Asia used industrial policies to affect the allocation of resources in ways that would stimulate economic growth. They took an entrepreneurial role in identifying industries in which research and development would have high payoffs. These governments intervened actively in the market; they used, complemented, regulated, and indeed created markets rather than supplanting them. They created an environment in which markets could thrive. These governments promoted exports, education, and technology; encouraged cooperation between government and industry and between firms and their workers; and at the same time, at least in some important sectors such as automobiles and electronics, encouraged competition. No single policy ensured success, nor did the absence of any single ingredient ensure failure. Why did governments undertake these policies? Why did politicians or bureaucrats not subvert them for their own self-interest? "The real miracle of East Asia may be more political than economic," Stiglitz asserts.[5]

East Asia was not the favored candidate for rapid economic growth during the 1950s. It had too many people and too few resources. Most observers favored the resource-rich African countries that were then moving towards independence. East Asia's development experience suggests that it is possible to catch up. Developing countries can move up the ladder. East Asia's experience is also a testament to the fact that countries with an authoritarian past can find a path to economic prosperity and democratic transition.

As successful as they are, East Asian economies are not immune to global economic crises. High savings rates in these nations have been considered one of the "secrets" to their success, but now East Asians are encouraged to spend more to stimulate domestic growth. As the global economic recession spread to the region in 2008 and 2009, East Asian governments were criticized by the West for not promoting domestic consumption despite the fact that cash had been distributed by some of these governments to encourage spending. The 2008–09 economic slump in East Asia also exposed the vulnerability of export-dependent economies. As cash-strapped Americans and Europeans decrease their demand for consumer goods, export sectors in East Asia have suffered tremendously. Shrinking demands in the West was also a cause of China's slower growth after 2010. To stimulate domestic consumption has become a new strategy in China's development.

The experience of Japan in the 1989–92 equity crash and the 1997 financial crisis tells us how costly avoiding financial reforms can be. Failure to recognize and address deep-seated structural problems in the financial sector and governance structure when they first emerged undermined confidence in economic management. The example of Japan also shows that structural reform remains a necessary condition for sustaining dynamic economic growth even at the most advanced economic level. After two decades of stagnation with only one previous prime minister, Koizumi Junichiro, making some structural reforms including the postal savings system, Japan finally began to tackle structural reforms seriously in the 2010s under the guidelines of Abenomics. As of the publication of this booklet, whether Japan's structural reforms will be successfully implemented in the near future is far from certain.

In its 1993 publication, *The East Asian Miracle: Economic Growth and Public Policy*, the World Bank listed a few factors that contributed to the success of East Asia's high performing economies: macroeconomic stability, limited and market-friendly government activism, strong promotion of export, rapid accumulation of human and physical capital, acquisition of advanced foreign technology, flexible labor markets, and "shared growth" in which the benefits of growth spread to all groups. In the twenty-first century, many of these economies are experiencing uneven development and income inequality, especially in China. A more sustainable and balanced development has become a key challenge to these economies. Development is not just economic growth but also involves quality of growth and justice in wealth distribution.

Not all roads lead to Rome. Developing countries that attempt to imitate East Asia's success may have to seek a development path most suitable for themselves based on their own histories, cultures, societies, and domestic and international environments. Which aspects of the East Asian "miracles" will work for other countries must be determined through pragmatic experimentation and adaptation based on local conditions.

NOTES

CHAPTER 2

[1] Ezra F. Vogel, *Japan as Number One: Lessons for America* (Cambridge, MA: Harvard University Press, 1979).

[2] Iokibe Makoto, "What was postwar Japanese diplomacy?" in *The Diplomatic History of Postwar Japan*, edited by Iokibe Makoto. Routledge, 2011: 212–14.

[3] Ming Wan, *The Political Economy of East Asia: Striving for Wealth and Power* (Washington, DC: Congressional Quarterly Press, 2008): 27.

[4] See http://en.wikipedia.org/wiki/Ikeda_Hayato.

[5] Chalmers Johnson, *MITI and the Japanese Miracle: The Growth of Industrial Policy 1925–1975* (Stanford, CA: Stanford University Press, 1982): viii.

[6] See T. J. Pempel, *Regime Shift: Comparative Dynamics of the Japanese Political Economy* (Ithaca, NY: Cornell University Press, 1998); Richard Katz, *Japan, the System That Soured: The Rise and Fall of the Japanese Economic Miracle* (Armonk, NY: M. E. Sharpe, 1998); and Meredith Woo-Cumings, ed., *The Developmental State* (Ithaca, NY: Cornell University Press, 1999).

[7] "U.S. Occupation Assistance: Iraq, Germany, and Japan Compared," Congressional Research Service, Library of Congress, Washington, DC, March 23, 2006.

[8] The Plaza Accord (or Plaza Agreement) was an agreement signed on September 22, 1985, at the Plaza Hotel in New York City by the ministers of finance and central bank governors of five nations: France, West Germany, Japan, the United States, and the United Kingdom. These five economies agreed to, among other things, depreciate the U.S. dollar in relation to the Japanese yen and German deutsche mark by intervening in currency markets. The exchange-rate value of the dollar versus the yen declined by 51 percent over the next two years. The signing of the Plaza Accord signified Japan's emergence as a real player in the global economy and the international monetary system.

[9] James R. Martin, "World Competitiveness Reports Summary," http://maaw.info/WorldCompetitivenessReports.htm.

[10] Ezra Vogel, *Is Japan Still Number One?* (Suban Jaya, Malaysia: Pelanduk Publications, 2001): 86.

[11] Edward J. Lincoln, "The Japanese Government and the Economy: Twenty-first Century Challenges," *Education About Asia* 12, no. 3 (winter 2007): 31–38.

CHAPTER 3

[1] Kwan S. Kim, "The Korean Miracle (1962–1980) Revisited: Myths and Realities in Strategy and Development," Working Papers, no. 166, University of Notre Dame, November 1991.

[2] Seymour Martin Lipset, "Some Social Requisites of Democracy: Economic Development and Political Legitimacy," *American Political Science Review* 53, no. 1 (March 1959): 69–105; Samuel P. Huntington, *Political Order in Changing Societies* (New Haven, CT: Yale University Press, 1968).

[3] David C. Kang, *Crony Capitalism: Corruption and Development in South Korea and the Philippines* (New York, NY: Cambridge University Press, 2002).

[4] Hagen Koo, ed., *State and Society in Contemporary Korea* (Ithaca, NY: Cornell University Press, 1993).

CHAPTER 4

[1] Thomas B. Gold, *State and Society in the Taiwan Miracle* (Armonk, NY: M. E. Sharpe, 1986): 125–26.

[2] Government Information Office, "The Story of Taiwan: Economy," www.taiwan.com.au/Polieco/History/ROC/report04.html (May 1, 2008). The Gini coefficient is a statistical measure of inequality of income distribution. It is defined as a ratio with values between zero and 1. A low Gini coefficient indicates more equal income or wealth distribution, while a high one indicates more unequal distribution. Zero corresponds to perfect equality (where everyone has the same income), and 1 corresponds to perfect inequality (where one person has all the income and everyone else has none).

[3] Lucien Ellington, "Taiwan in the Classroom: Economic Freedom, Political Freedom, International Pariah?" *Virginia Review of Asian Studies*, 15(1), spring 2013: 1–10

[4] Ambassador Chas W. Freeman, Jr. (USFS, Ret.), "China and the Economic Integration of Europe and Asia," Remarks to the Summer Roundtable of the Pacific Pension Institute, San Francisco, California, July 23, 2015.

[5] These three paragraphs are adapted from "Key Issues in China's Economic Transformation," United Nations Conference on Trade and Development (UNCTAD), www.unctad.org.

[6] Orville Schell, "The Enigma of China's Economic 'Miracle,'" *AsiaMedia*, November 1, 2003.

CHAPTER 5

[1] "China's Miracle," *Star* (Malaysia), March 20, 2008.

[2] Tom Ginsburg, "Democratic Transitions: Case Studies from Asia," Foreign Policy Research Institute E-Notes, http://www.fpri.org, December 19, 2007.

[3] T. J. Pempel, "Revisiting the Japanese Economic Model," in *Japan and China in the World Political Economy*, edited by Saadia M. Pekkanen and Kellee S. Tsai (London and New York: Routledge, 2005): 35–36.

[4] Political scientist Samuel P. Huntington in T*he Third Wave: Democratization in the Late Twentieth Century* (Norman, OK: University of Oklahoma Press, 1993), used the term "the third wave of democratization" to refer to the global trend between 1974 and 1990 when approximately thirty countries, from Southern and Eastern Europe to Latin America and Asia, made the transition to democracy. The first wave brought democracy to Western Europe and North America in the eighteenth and nineteenth centuries. The second wave began after World War II but lost steam in the 1960s.

CHAPTER 6

[1] Paul Krugman, "The Myth of Asia's Miracle," *Foreign Affairs* 73, no. 6 (November–December 1994): 62–78.

[2] Paul Krugman, "What Ever Happened to the Asian Miracle?" *Fortune* 136 (4), 1997: 27.

[3] Masahiko Aoki et al., eds., *The Role of Government in East Asian Economic Development: Comparative Institutional Analysis* (New York, NY: Oxford University Press, 1998); Robert Wade, *Governing the Market: Economic Theory and the Role of Government in East Asian Industrialization* (Princeton, NJ: Princeton University Press, 2003).

[4] Richard Stubbs, *Rethinking Asia's Economic Miracle* (New York: Palgrave-Macmillan, 2005).The American sociologist and political scientist Charles Tilly first proposed the thesis that states make war and wars make states in *Coercion, Capital, and European States: A.D. 990–1992* (Malden, MA: Blackwell, 1993).

[5] Joseph Stiglitz, "Some Lessons from the East Asian Miracle," *World Bank Research Observer* 11, no. 2 (August 1996): 175.

GLOSSARY

Abenomics: Economic policies advocated by Abe Shinzō since December 2012 when he began his second term as prime minister of Japan. Abenomics has three pillars or "three arrows": fiscal stimulus, monetary easing and structural reforms. Under the policies, the Japanese yen weakened and consumption tax was increased. With a lower unemployment rate, the Japanese economy experienced moderate recovery but deep seated structural problems remain.

AIIB: Asian Infrastructure Investment Bank. A China-initiated investment bank set up in 2015 that aims at providing investments for developing countries especially in infrastructure. Many consider it a complement to the existing international financial institutions such as the World Bank, International Monetary Fund, and Asian Development Bank. Some consider it as a rival to these institutions.

Beijing Consensus: A term coined by Joshua Cooper Ramo in a 2004 article that describes an alternative economic development model to the Washington Consensus of market-friendly policies promoted by the IMF, World Bank and U.S. Treasury. Sometimes used interchangeably with "the China model" or "the China experience," which is characterized by a largely free-market economy under authoritarian political control.

Byungjin: Parallel development. A policy in North Korea under the leadership of Kim Jong-un that emphasizes both economic growth and nuclear development. Many consider it an unsustainable policy.

Century of humiliation: Roughly beginning from the first Opium War in 1839 and ending in 1949 with the founding of the PRC. A period in which a weak China suffered from Western and Japanese domination. It still shapes Chinese mindsets and foreign policy.

Chaebol: The South Korean form of business conglomerates. They are global multinationals owning numerous international enterprises. There are several dozen such large family-controlled corporate groups. Through aggressive governmental support and finance, some have become well-known international brand names, such as Samsung, Hyundai, Daewoo, and LG.

Crony capitalism: A pejorative term for an allegedly capitalist economy in which success in business depends on close relationships between business people and government officials. It is typified by favoritism in the distribution of legal contracts, government grants, special tax breaks, and so on.

Dodge plan or Dodge line: Efforts to stimulate postwar economic recovery in Japan. Named after Joseph Dodge, chairman of the Detroit Bank, who went to Japan in 1948 as an economic adviser to help devise an austerity program and achieve a balanced budget for Japan.

Developmental state: A term used by international political economy scholars to refer to state-led macroeconomic planning in East Asia in the twentieth century. In this model of capitalism, the state has more independent, or autonomous, political power and more control over the economy. A developmental state is characterized by having strong state intervention and extensive regulation and planning.

ECFA: The Economic Cooperation Framework Agreement signed by Taiwan and mainland China in 2010. The first such formal trade agreement between the two sides since 1949.

Four "little dragons": or **four "little tigers,"** which refers to the rapidly-industrializing economies of Hong Kong, Taiwan, Singapore and South Korea between the 1960s and the 1990s.

Fukoku kyohei: "Enrich the country, strengthen the military," Japan's national slogan during the Meiji era.

Iron triangle: A term used to describe the close relationship among conservative LDP politicians, big businesses, and elite bureaucrats in post-World War II Japan.

Kangsong taeguk: "A strong and prosperous great state." It was Kim Jong-il's vision to modernize North Korea. With his death at the end of 2011, it is unclear how the North Korean regime, under his son Kim Jong-un's leadership, will realize this dream.

Keiretsu: Close interlocking structure of suppliers, manufacturers and distributors, usually centered on a large financial institution. Such business groups maintained dominance over the Japanese economy for the greater half of the twentieth century.

Meiji Restoration: A chain of events that restored imperial rule to Japan beginning in 1868. The Restoration led to enormous changes in Japan's political and social structure, ushering in a period of rapid industrialization and modernization of Japan. The Meiji era extended from September 1868 through July 1912, during which Japanese society moved from isolated feudalism to its modern form.

OECD: Organization for Economic Cooperation and Development. 18 developed European countries plus the United States and Canada created this organization in 1960 dedicated to global development. Japan became a member in 1964, and South Korea 1996.

One Belt, One Road: Unveiled by President Xi Jinping in 2013, they are China's new development strategies. The land-based "Silk Road Economic Belt" and the oceangoing "Maritime Silk Road" connect China with Central Asia, the Mediterranean, Europe, Southeast Asia, South Asia, and East Africa and promote China's economic cooperation with countries along the routes.

Plaza Accord or Plaza Agreement: An agreement between the governments of France, West Germany, Japan, the United States, and the United Kingdom, to depreciate the U.S. dollar in relation to the Japanese yen and German Deutsche Mark by intervening in currency markets. The five governments signed the accord on September 22, 1985 at the Plaza Hotel in New York City. It reflected Japan's emergence as a real player in managing the international monetary system. It is also postulated that the accord contributed to the Japanese asset price bubble, which ended up in a serious recession, from which Japan has not fully recovered.

Resource curse: the paradox that countries with an abundance of natural resources tend to have less economic growth than countries without these natural resources.

SCAP: Supreme Commander of the Allied Powers. The title held by General Douglas MacArthur during the Occupation of Japan following World War II. SCAP played a crucial role in Japan's initial economic recovery.

Shushin koyo: Lifetime employment. Common in the Japanese work environment where advancement is based on seniority and there is a close bond between employees and the employer. Such practice has been challenged by Japan's economic malaise since the 1990s.

Special Economic Zone (SEZ): A geographical region that has economic and other laws more free-market-oriented than a country's national laws. In China, Deng Xiaoping initiated reform policies in 1979 and established four such SEZs on the southeast coast of China, which include Shenzhen, Xiamen, Zhuhai, and Shantou. These small and sleepy towns were quickly transformed into modern metropolises thanks to preferential policies they enjoyed.

Taiwan Relations Act (TRA): A U.S. law passed in 1979 to govern U.S.-Taiwan relations following the U.S. government's decision to switch diplomatic recognition from Taipei to Beijing.

The 1955 system: Refers to the domination of the Liberal Democratic Party (LDP) in Japanese politics from 1955 to 1993.

Three Principles of the People (*sanmin zhuyi*): Developed by Dr. Sun Yat-sen in the early 20th century as part of a philosophy to make China a free, prosperous, and powerful nation. They include the principle of Minzu (nationalism), the principle of Minquan (people's power), and the principle of Minsheng (people's livelihood).

Trans-Pacific Partnership (TPP): A US-led free trade agreement involving twelve Pacific Rim nations. It seeks to lower trade barriers, establish a common framework for intellectual property, enforce standards for labor and environmental laws, and establish an investor-state dispute settlement mechanism. The agreement was reached in Atlanta, USA in October 2015. Japan is a member, with South Korea, Taiwan, and the PRC hoping to join at a later date.

Yin jin lai: "to bring in," China's strategy, especially during the 1980s and 1990s, to attract foreign investment and technology.

Yoshida Doctrine: Named after Japan's post-World War II Prime Minister Yoshida Shigeru, who placed highest national priority on economic development while simultaneously keeping a low profile in foreign affairs. Relying on the United States for security, Japan was able to recover quickly. It guided Japan's postwar reconstruction.

Zou chu qu: "to go out," China's new "going global" strategy in the 21st century of investing and purchasing abroad as its economy becomes stronger and its businesses more globally competitive.

Suggestions for Further Reading

Adams, F. Gerard, and Shinichi Ichimura, eds. *East Asian Development: Will the East Asian Miracle Growth Survive?* Westport, CT: Praeger, 1998.

Amsden, Alice. *Asia's Next Giant: South Korea and the Late Industrialization.* Oxford: Oxford University Press, 1989.

Amyx, Jennifer A. *Japan's Financial Crisis: Institutional Rigidity and Reluctant Change.* Princeton: Princeton University Press, 2004.

Armstrong, Charles K. *Tyranny of the Weak: North Korea and the World 1950–1992* (Cornell University Press, 2013).

Aoki, Masahiko, Hyung-Ki Kim, and Masahiro Okuno-Fujiwara, eds. *The Role of Government in East Asian Economic Development: Comparative Institutional Analysis.* Oxford: Oxford University Press, 1998.

Ash, Robert, John W. Garver and Penelope Prime, eds. *Taiwan's Democracy: Economic and Political Challenges.* London and New York: Routledge, 2011.

Bende-Nabende, Anthony, ed. *International Trade, Capital Flows, and Economic Development in East Asia: The Challenge in the Twenty-first Century.* Hampshire: Ashgate, 2003.

Berger, Peter L., and Michael Hsin-huang Hsiao, eds. *In Search of an East Asian Development Model.* New Brunswick, NJ: Transaction, 1988.

Bramall, Chris. *Chinese Economic Development.* London and New York: Routledge, 2008.

Breslin, Shaun, ed. *East Asia and the Global Crisis.* London and New York: Routledge, 2012.

Brødsgaard, Kjeld Erik, and Susan Young, eds. *State Capacity in East Asia: Japan, Taiwan, China, and Vietnam.* New York: Oxford University Press, 2000.

Campos, Jose Edgardo, and Hilton L. Root. *The Key to the Asian Miracle: Making Shared Growth Credible.* Washington, DC: Brookings Institution, 1996.

Chan, Steve, Cal Clark, and Danny Lam, eds. *Beyond the Developmental State: East Asia's Political Economies Reconsidered.* New York: St. Martin's, 1998.

Chang, Ha-Joon. *The East Asian Development Experience: The Miracle, the Crisis, and the Future.* London and New York: Zed, 2007.

Cheung, Yin-Wong and Guonan Ma, eds. *Asia and China in the Global Economy.* Singapore: World Scientific Publishing, 2011.

Cohen, Warren I. *East Asia at the Center: Four Thousand Years of Engagement with the World.* New York: Columbia University Press, 2000.

Das, Dilip K. *The Asian Economy: Spearheading the Recovery from the Global Financial Crisis.* London and New York: Routledge, 2011.

Deyo, Fred, ed. *The Political Economy of the New Asian Industrialism.* Ithaca: Cornell University Press, 1987.

Dickson, Bruce J. *Democratization in China and Taiwan: The Adaptability of Leninist Parties.* New York: Oxford University Press, 1997.

———. *Red Capitalists in China: The Party, Private Entrepreneurs, and Prospects for Political Change.* New York: Columbia University Press, 2003.

Drysdale, Peter. *Reform and Recovery in East Asia: The Role of the State and Economic Enterprise.* London and New York: Routledge, 2000.

Flynn, Norman. *Miracle to Meltdown in Asia: Business, Government, and Society.* Oxford: Oxford University Press, 1999.

Forsberg, Aaron. *America and the Japanese Miracle: The Cold War Context of Japan's Postwar Economic Revival, 1950–1960.* Chapel Hill: University of North Carolina Press, 2000.

Francks, Penelope. *Japanese Economic Development: Theory and Practice.* London and New York: Routledge, 1992.

Garnaut, Ross and Ligang Song, eds. *The China Boom and Its Discontents.* Australia National University Press, 2012.

Gaston, Noel, ed. *Economic and Policy Developments in East Asia.* London and New York: Routledge, 2015.

Ginsburg, Tom. "Democratic Transitions: Case Studies from Asia." *Foreign Policy Research Institute E-Notes,* http://www.fpri.org, December 1, 2007.

Glick, Reuven, and Ramon Moreno. "The East Asian Miracle: Growth Because of Government Intervention and Protectionism or in Spite of It?" *Business Economics,* Vol. 32:2 (April 1997): 20–25.

Gold, Thomas B. *State and Society in the Taiwan Miracle.* Armonk, NY: M. E. Sharpe, 1986.

Goldstein, Morris. *The Asian Financial Crisis: Causes, Cures, and Systemic Implications.* Washington, DC: Institute for International Economics, 1998.

Haggard, Stephan. *Pathways from the Periphery: Politics of Growth in the Newly Industrializing Countries.* Ithaca: Cornell University Press, 1990.

———. "Institutions and Growth in East Asia." *Studies in Comparative International Development* 38 (4), 2004: 53–81.

Hamada, Koichi, Keijiro Otsuka, Gustav Ranis, and Ken Togo. *Miraculous Growth and Stagnation in Post-War Japan.* London and New York: Routledge, 2011.

Harrison, Lawrence E., and Samuel P. Huntington, eds. *Culture Matters: How Values Shape Human Progress.* New York: Basic Books, 2000.

Henderson, Jeffrey. *East Asian Transformation: On the Political Economy of Dynamism, Governance and Crisis.* London and New York: Routledge, 2011.

Hira, Anil. *An East Asian Model for Latin American Success: The New Path.* Hampshire: Ashgate, 2007.

Howe, Brendan M. ed. *Post-Conflict Development in East Asia.* Burlington, VT: Ashgate, 2014.

Hsueh, Li-min, Chen-kuo Hsu, and Dwight H. Perkins. *Industrialization and the State: The Changing Role of the Taiwan Government in the Economy, 1945–1998.* Cambridge: Harvard Institute for International Development, 2001.

Hua, Shiping, and Hu Ruihua, eds. *East Asian Development Model: Twenty-first century perspectives.* London and New York: Routledge, 2014.

Huang, Yasheng. *Selling China: Foreign Direct Investment during the Reform Era.* Cambridge: Cambridge University Press, 2003.

———. "Rethinking the Beijing Consensus," *Asia Policy* 11 (2011): 1–26.

Hughes, Helen, ed. *Achieving Industrialization in East Asia.* Cambridge: Cambridge University Press, 1988.

Ikeo, Aiko. *Economic Development in Twentieth-Century East Asia: The International Context.* London and New York: Routledge, 1997.

Iokibe, Makoto, and Robert D. Eldridge, eds. *The Diplomatic History of Postwar Japan.* London and New York: Routledge, 2011.

Islam, Iyanatul, and Anis Chowdhury. *The Political Economy of East Asia: Post-Crisis Debates.* Oxford: Oxford University Press, 2000.

Ito, Takatoshi, and Anne O. Krueger, eds. *Growth Theories in Light of the East Asian Experience.* Chicago: University of Chicago Press, 1995.

———. *The Role of Foreign Direct Investment in East Asian Economic Development.* Chicago: University of Chicago Press, 2000.

Jackson, Karl D., ed. *Asian Contagion: The Causes and Consequences of a Financial Crisis.* Boulder: Westview, 1999.

Johnson, Chalmers. *MITI and the Japanese Miracle: The Growth of Industrial Policy, 1925–1975.* Stanford: Stanford University Press, 1982.

Kang, David C. *Crony Capitalism: Corruption and Development in South Korea and the Philippines.* New York: Cambridge University Press, 2002.

Kato, Takatoshi. "Can the East Asian Miracle Persist?" Speech delivered at Princeton University, December 2, 2004; http://www.imf.org/external/np/speeches/2004/120204.htm.

Katz, Richard. *Japan: The System That Soured—the Rise and Fall of the Japanese Economic Miracle.* Armonk, NY: M. E. Sharpe, 1998.

———. *Japanese Phoenix: The Long Road to Economic Revival.* Armonk, NY: M. E. Sharpe, 2002.

Katzenstein, Peter. *A World of Regions: Asia and Europe in the American Imperium.* Ithaca: Cornell University Press, 2005.

Kim, Kwan S. "The Korean Miracle (1962–1980) Revisited: Myths and Realities in Strategy and Development." Working Papers, no. 166, University of Notre Dame, November 1991.

Kim, Mason M. S. *Comparative Welfare Capitalism in East Asia: Productivist Models of Social Policy.* New York: Palgrave Macmillan, 2015.

Kim, Samuel S., ed. *East Asia and Globalization.* Lanham, MD: Rowman and Littlefield, 2000.

Koo, Hagen, ed. *State and Society in Contemporary Korea.* Ithaca: Cornell University Press, 1993.

Koo, Richard C. *The Holy Grail of Macroeconomics: Lessons from Japan's Great Recession.* Singapore: John Wiley and Sons (Asia), 2009.

Krugman, Paul. "The Myth of Asia's Miracle." *Foreign Affairs* 73, no. 6 (November–December 1994): 62–78.

———. "What Ever Happened to the Asian Miracle?" *Fortune* 136 (4), 1997: 26–29.

Lee, Kuan Yew. *The Singapore Story: Memoirs of Lee Kuan Yew.* Singapore: Prentice Hall, 1998.

Lee, You-Il. *From Evolution to Revolution: Korea's New Market Environment.* Hampshire: Ashgate, 2003.

Liao, Jessica Chia-yueh. *Developmental States and Business Activism: East Asia's Trade Dispute Settlement.* New York: Palgrave Macmillan, 2016.

Lin, Justin Yifu. *Demystifying The Chinese Economy.* Cambridge: Cambridge University Press, 2011.

Lin, Justin Yifu, Fang Cai, and Zhou Li. *The China Miracle: Development Strategy and Economic Reform.* Hong Kong: Chinese University Press, 1996.

Lipset, Seymour Martin. "Some Social Requisites of Democracy: Economic Development and Political Legitimacy." *American Political Science Review* 53, no. 1 (March 1959): 69–105.

Lye, Liang Fook and Chen Gang, eds. *Towards a Liveable and Sustainable Urban Environment: Eco-Cities in East Asia.* Singapore: World Scientific Publishing, 2010.

Nissanke, Machiko, and Ernest Aryeetey, eds. *Comparative Development Experiences of Sub-Saharan Africa and East Asia: An Institutional Approach.* Hampshire: Ashgate, 2003.

Nolan, Peter. "Globalization and Industrial Policy: The Case of China." *The World Economy* 37 (6), 2014: 747–764.

OECD. *OECD Economic Surveys* (*on Japan and Korea*), OECD Publishing, various years.

Park, Bae-Gyoon, Richard Child Hill, and Asato Saito, eds. *Locating Neoliberalism in East Asia: Neoliberalizing Spaces in Developmental States.* New York: Wiley-Blackwell, 2012.

Pascua, Arthur. *Devastation in Japan: An Economic Analysis.* Seattle, WA: CreateSpace, 2012.

Pei, Minxin. *China's Trapped Transition: The Limits of Developmental Autocracy.* Cambridge: Harvard University Press, 2006.

Pekkanen, Saadia M., and Kellee S. Tsai, eds. *Japan and China in the World Political Economy.* London and New York: Routledge, 2005.

Pempel, T. J. *Regime Shift: Comparative Dynamics of the Japanese Political Economy.* Ithaca: Cornell University Press, 1998.

———. *The Politics of the Asian Economic Crisis.* Ithaca: Cornell University Press, 1999.

Pempel, T. J., ed. *Remapping East Asia: The Construction of a Region.* Ithaca: Cornell University Press, 2004.

Perkins, Dwight H. *East Asian Development: Foundations and Strategies.* Cambridge, MA: Harvard University Press, 2013.

Petri, Peter A. *The Lessons of East Asia: Common Foundations of East Asian Success*. Washington, DC: World Bank, 1993.

Przeworski, Adam. *States and Markets: A Primer in Political Economy.* Cambridge: Cambridge University Press, 2003.

Ramo, Joshua Cooper. *The Beijing Consensus.* London: Foreign Policy Center, 2004.

Schaede, Ulrike. "What Happened to the Japanese Model?" *Review of International Economics* 12 (2), 2004: 277–294.

Schell, Orville. "The Enigma of China's Economic 'Miracle.'" *AsiaMedia* (UCLA Asia Institute), November 1, 2003.

Stiglitz, Joseph. "Some Lessons from the East Asian Miracle." *World Bank Research Observer* 11, no. 2 (August 1996): 151–77.

Stiglitz, Joseph, and Shahid Yusuf. *Rethinking the East Asian Miracle.* Washington, DC: World Bank, 2001.

Stubbs, Richard. *Rethinking Asia's Economic Miracle.* New York: Palgrave-Macmillan, 2005.

Sugihara, Kaoru, ed. *Japan, China, and the Growth of the Asian International Political Economy, 1850–1949.* Oxford: Oxford University Press, 2005.

Thirlwall, A.P. *Economics of Development: Theory and Evidence,* 9th edition. New York: Palgrave Macmillan, 2011.

Tilly, Charles. *Coercion, Capital, and European States, A.D. 990–1992.* Malden, MA: Blackwell, 1993.

Toyoda, Toshihisa, Hiroshi Kan Sato, and Jun Nishikawa, eds. *Economic and Policy Lessons from Japan to Developing Countries.* New York: Palgrave Macmillan, 2011.

Vogel, Ezra. *Japan as Number One: Lessons for America.* Cambridge: Harvard University Press, 1979.

———. *Is Japan Still Number One?* Suban Jaya: Pelanduk, 2001.

Vogel, Steven K. *Japan Remodeled: How Government and Industry Are Reforming Japanese Capitalism.* Ithaca: Cornell University Press, 2006.

Wade, Robert. *Governing the Market: Economic Theory and the Role of Government in East Asian Industrialization.* Princeton: Princeton University Press, 2003.

Wan, Ming. *The Political Economy of East Asia: Striving for Wealth and Power.* Washington, DC: Congressional Quarterly Press, 2008.

―――. *The Asian Infrastructure Investment Bank: The Construction of Power and the Struggle for the East Asian International Order.* New York: Palgrave Macmillan, 2016.

Wang, Shaoguang, and Angang Hu. *The Political Economy of Uneven Development: The Case of China.* Armonk, NY: M. E. Sharpe, 1999.

Whang, I-J. "The Role of Government in Economic Development: The Korean Experience." *Asian Development Review* 5, no. 2 (1987): 70–87.

Woo-Cumings, Meredith. ed. *The Developmental State.* Ithaca: Cornell University Press, 1999.

World Bank. *East Asia: Recovery and Beyond.* Washington, DC, 2000.

―――. *The East Asian Miracle: Economic Growth and Public Policy.* Washington, DC, 1993.

Zhu, Zhiqun. ed. *New Dynamics in East Asian Politics: Security, Political Economy, and Society.* New York and London: Continuum International, 2012.

―――. ed. *Globalization, Development and Security in Asia.* World Scientific Publishing, 2014.

Zoellick, Robert. "Economics and Security in the Changing Asia-Pacific." *Survival* 39, no. 4 (winter 1997–98): 29–51.